PERSONAL LEARNING
NETWORKS

PERSONAL LEARNING NETWORKS

Professional Development for the Isolated School Librarian

Mary Ann Harlan

A Member of the Greenwood Publishing Group

Westport, Connecticut • London

Library of Congress Cataloging-in-Publication Data

Harlan, Mary Ann.
  Personal learning networks : professional development for the isolated school librarian / Mary Ann Harlan.
    p. cm.
  Includes bibliographical references and index.
  ISBN 978–1–59158–790–3 (alk. paper)
  1. School librarians—Education (Continuing education)   2. Teacher-librarians—Education (Continuing education)   3. School librarians—In-service training.   4. Teacher-librarians—In-service training.   5. School librarians—Professional relationships.   6. Teacher-librarians—Professional relationships. 7. Library education (Continuing education)   8. Library science—Computer network resources.   9. Career development.   10. Self-culture.   I. Title.
  Z682.4.S34H37   2009
  027.8—dc22   2008045519

British Library Cataloguing in Publication Data is available.

Library of Congress Catalog Card Number: 2008045519
ISBN: 978–1–59158–790–3

First published in 2009

Libraries Unlimited, 88 Post Road West, Westport, CT 06881
A Member of the Greenwood Publishing Group, Inc.
www.lu.com

Printed in the United States of America

The paper used in this book complies with the
Permanent Paper Standard issued by the National
Information Standards Organization (Z39.48–1984).

10 9 8 7 6 5 4 3 2 1

Copyright Acknowledgments

Screenshots from Diigo, LibraryThing, and Goodreads used with permission.

Contents

Introduction

When I was first introduced to blogs and wikis several years ago I immediately saw the implications for my high school library. The tools increased the possibilities of communicating and collaborating with the community, staff, students, and parents who I served. This provides interesting new possibilities for curriculum. What I was unprepared for at the time was the impact Web 2.0 would have on my own personal growth as a teacher-librarian.

As I became more comfortable using tools and exploring resources I discovered blogs from writers I enjoyed, teacher-librarians I respected, and sources that expanded my vision for collection development. I "lurked" on wiki sites, and tried out the tools and resources they recommended. When I heard about the "next big thing" whether it was Twitter or a Ning, I spent time trying the tools. Some ideas caught on immediately, others I have never used regularly (although many teacher-librarians do).

When I discovered, and set up my first RSS reader, I turned a corner in the Web 2.0 environment. Here was a way to immediately access the variety of material that I was struggling to find time to incorporate into my day. Sometimes I would remember to visit a site, other days I was much too busy. An RSS reader immediately solved this problem, saving new posts until I had time.

What I discovered is that Web 2.0 tools were contributing to my professional growth. I learned about new ideas, read about effective practices, stayed on top of what was popular in teenagers' literary world and other popular culture such as television, movies, and music. Yes, the tools played a role in the library program. I integrated wikis, wrote a blog, and provided an IM reference service during the school days, and evening hours. But I learned about IM reference (specifically Meebo) from an ed-tech blog I read on a regular basis. And I was learning so much more. I "met" teacher-librarians and youth service librarians who I respected because of their knowledge and passion for their jobs. I stepped outside of the library, and read ed-tech blogs that introduced new tools, and was reminded how much technology coordinators and teachers have in common with teacher-librarians; occasionally they are the same person.

Instantly, I became much more connected to the educational world, across all 50 states, and several countries. Although I may not be instantly recognizable to those who share their ideas and thoughts, I am grateful for the opportunity to learn from them. I have taken more risks, improved my program, and achieved more than I could have had I not entered this world. It was well worth the exploratory time I spent one summer, and the time spent maintaining the network of people and sites I consider a part of my personal learning network.

This book is meant to be a handbook for those wishing to explore the possibilities of Web 2.0 for their professional growth. It was written with the "newbie" in mind, someone entering this environment for the first time, but hopefully those comfortable in this environment also will find something new, a fresh idea, for their personal learning network.

CHAPTER 1
Personal Learning Networks

This chapter explores what has come to be known as personal learning networks (PLNs). Once you understand the definition you may find that you already have a PLN, or perhaps you don't. Once you understand the description of a PLN, it will be easy to recognize its value.

PERSONAL LEARNING NETWORKS: A DEFINITION

What is a PLN? Put simply, it is the people with whom you surround yourself, the tools you use, and the resources you rely on to introduce yourself to new ideas and best practices. It is a network that encourages learning and personal growth. For many teachers, their PLN does not expand beyond their school staff. For teacher-librarians, PLNs can be more complicated because of our relative isolation and the singular nature of our position within a staff. Out of necessity, the global learning network for teacher-librarians has grown to be a thriving community. A PLN built from that global community can provide a teacher-librarian with access to professional development and a connection to members of their profession well beyond their immediate location.

Often, there is only one teacher-librarian in the building, perhaps the only one in the district, or even the county. We are isolated in ways that other disciplines are not. In staff rooms and teacher's meetings, our colleagues can discuss the growing disaffection among math students with other math teachers, or members of the English department can discuss

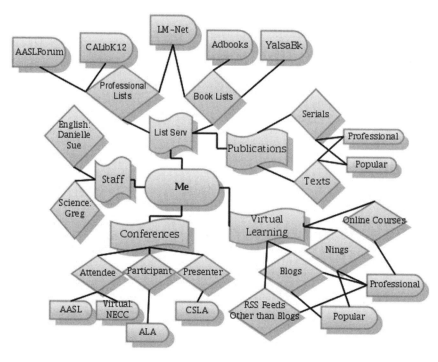

Figure 1.1 A graphic representation of a personal learning network.

the impact of texting on academic writing in the English classroom. Teacher-librarians may join with the elective teachers or other specialists to discuss the impact of No Child Left Behind (NCLB) on our programs, but we cannot discuss the most recent techniques in teaching art, or the impact of class size on a project-based classroom such as the woodshop. We may even find ourselves in competition with other specialists for the paucity of funds. We may be lucky enough to work with teachers who stay current on children's or young adult literature (although in my experience it is a rare teacher who reads what his or her students read), but quite often we do not. In terms of sharing effective practices, a thorough discussion of information literacy standards from the American Association of School Librarians (AASL), the International Society for Technology in Education (ISTE), and/or the Association of College and Research Libraries (ACRL), or discussing current thought on the integration of technology in the school library, we may be on our own.

Working in this environment has led to the creation of communities of similarly isolated school librarians, and the evolution of virtual environment has provided an opportunity for teacher-librarians to participate in a professional development with other teacher-librarians. We are able to ask questions, discuss, and share in a global community. This provides many opportunities for life-long learning, both within our field, and in other fields that provide insight into what it is we do. One only has to look.

Figure 1.1 is a diagram of my PLN. It highlights the tools that work for me. Each learning network will look different, as they are customizable for each user. Some teacher-librarians may find traveling to conferences difficult and prohibitively costly. Others may find a particular virtual community overwhelming, or not particularly focused. Each of us can start in the center and discover different elements of the world beyond our walls that enhance our learning, and therefore our working environment.

Perhaps you are a "newbie" teacher-librarian, starting your first job and nervous and overwhelmed about what you might not have learned in school. Perhaps you have your feet under you and now you are trying to stay ahead of the curve in terms of effective practices for teacher-librarians. Perhaps you have been working for quite some time and you take pride in staying up to date in the profession. The goal of this book is to provide a place to start when looking for communities that provide support and professional development, as well as ways to contribute. It should help you extend your PLN. We all have something to share, and in the 21st Century, that is easier than ever to do.

In the next chapter, I investigate the particulars of professional development for teacher-librarians. Professional development in the school library has a slightly different focus than that of a subject area teacher, particularly a core subject area such as English or math.

CHAPTER 2
Professional Development

In this chapter, I examine why professional development is so fundamental to a teacher-librarian's success. The demands on education, and particularly on library programs are multifaceted, and those of us working in school libraries need to be prepared to respond.

WHY PROFESSIONAL DEVELOPMENT?

The first and most obvious answer is that states and districts require a certain amount of professional development. These requirements are imposed because it is important that teachers and teacher-librarians continue learning. Although we have completed our formal education and have been certified as teachers, it is not enough. Even though when we walk into our classrooms each day, we are learning, it is not enough. Learning is a life long proposition, and to be our best in the classroom we should look beyond our classroom walls, and continue to encounter new and challenging ideas.

Our world and the world of our students are constantly changing. We live in a more global society than we did even 20 years ago. Our students have access to tools that open the world up to them far beyond their hometown and in ways that educators could not have imagined a century ago. New research, and old politics, make demands on educators who must be willing to adjust to NCLB, project-based learning, Bloom's taxonomies, Gardner's intelligences, literacy initiatives,

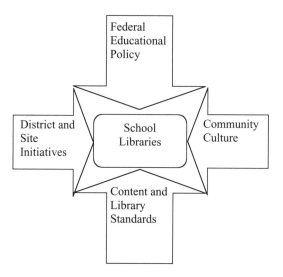

Figure 2.1 Forces acting on school libraries.

second-language learners, and the other laws and educational theories that come our way (see Figure 2.1).

Our classrooms, and our libraries, are changing and will continue to change in ways we cannot yet imagine, and yet, in many respects, they remain the same. This makes it the responsibility of teachers and teacher-librarians, who must grow and change, to adapt to the children who cross our thresholds and to the standards of our disciplines as new research, new tools, and new ideas impact our understanding of our subjects. As teachers and as citizens, we are lifelong learners, modeling the same for our students. And so the ability to develop a network and to implement strategies to keep learning throughout our careers is an essential part of our profession.

As mentioned previously, teacher-librarians may find themselves isolated within their school, district, or even county. A PLN can help relieve that isolation and open up communication with other teacher-librarians who are struggling with similar isolation and who have the same concerns and interests you do. The old adage that two heads are better than one is multiplied with the ability to turn to the thousands of "heads" represented by the national list, LM_Net, which is dedicated to school library media specialists worldwide, and to people involved with the school library media field, or other state listservs. This is very reassuring.

Many more communities exist in our virtual landscape. They represent particular interests, passions, or needs that will help alleviate the feeling of isolation. By seeking out professional development and bringing best practices and fresh ideas to your staff, you can become a leader on your campus.

Even if leadership is not a natural role for you, the PLN you have created will offer support and confidence, and you may find yourself in an unexpected role. As a leader on campus you begin to cement the importance of your program, and the teacher-librarian's role within a campus, a strong advocacy position.

CURRENCY

Currency is perhaps the biggest reason to establish a PLN that expands beyond your immediate circumstance, and that can provide learning opportunities. It can be difficult to keep up with the ever-changing world. Technology has been changing at a remarkable rate. Within many teacher-librarians' careers, we have seen the Internet grow from a creation in the world of computer science (and beyond our ability to understand) to a vibrant, wild community with which we wrestle daily and without its use, we cannot quite conceive of our job. (Especially true if we have never worked without it.) As we move beyond audio-visual equipment, teacher-librarians find themselves in the position of using new equipment, new software, and integrating new technological tools into programs and lessons. Teacher-librarians often are the "technology gurus" on campuses and are training other staff on software and hardware.

We use Web sites, wikis, online cataloging, e-mail, instant messaging (IM), and other tools to deliver services. Staying ahead of the curve with recommendations, integration, and experimentation is a vital part of our job.

Teacher-librarians must also stay aware of current and changing education trends, which is not an easy task. Education has been subject to the perennial swing of the pendulum and schools seem to be back into rote learning. The recent laws of NCLB and high-stakes standardized testing are a reaction to the portfolio-based, alternative assessments of the years prior. Often teacher-librarians are left out of current educational debates upon which the library has a direct impact. As an example, the current debate over literacy often is taking place without the voice of teacher-librarians. It is imperative that teacher-librarians be aware of the language of the literacy debate and find a place within the debate for school libraries. Teacher-librarians must encourage literacy coaches, teachers, and administrators to consider the school library as the center of a schoolwide literacy program. Although educational debates may be based on former arguments regarding the "best" educational approach and have their roots in Ancient Greece and Socrates, the impact of the educational pendulum on our library programs remains. We cannot dismiss the swing of the pendulum with the attitude that this current trend will soon be displaced by another. Being aware and proactive in engaging in any debate, highlighting the role of the library in the lives of the students within the context of current educational policy is important. We must consider current policies and educational trends while making decisions regarding library and information literacy programs and teaching. We cannot make truly informed decisions without current awareness of the context of educational policies.

It is not just in technology implementation and the educational debate that awareness of the most current thinking is important. The publishing industry in children's and young adult materials has boomed and we are seeing a new "Golden Age" of literature for students. When Harry Potter finds himself on the cover of *Time* magazine and the Gossip Girl series is debated in *The New York Times*, teacher-librarians also must be aware of the titles, the debates, and the accolades surrounding literature for children and young adults.

It goes beyond the popular titles, and those that find their way into mainstream media. As advocates of literacy and reading, teacher-librarians have a unique opportunity to help students experience literature, not because it is assigned for a class but because they derive pleasure from reading. School libraries may well be the last place in a child's educational career that not only supports, but also encourages, reading for pleasure. In order to match the right student with the right book, it helps to be aware of current trends in reading, newly published material, as well as the perennial favorites. Some of these may be considered controversial, and a wise teacher-librarian has considered these controversies and is well prepared. Being aware of, prepared for, and having considered the debates surrounding books such as *And Tango Makes Three*, the Gossip Girl series, and *The Golden Compass* will assist in any potential concerns on the part of parents and administrators who have become aware of the controversies, but have not yet read the titles. Keeping current with children's and young adult literature cannot be overlooked as a fundamental part of professional development for teacher-librarians.

Meanwhile, students experience new fads, fashions, and popular culture. Just who are the Jonas Brothers, Robert Pattison, and Kristen Stewart or Judd Apatow and his merry band of actors? And how can popular culture find a way into our programs, or should it? If we are to encourage reading for pleasure it helps to have a passing knowledge of the popular culture that our children, "tweens," and teens are encountering. If we know what is popular and provide reading materials that enhance student understanding or enjoyment, the library becomes a place cemented in their minds as one where they can find interesting and valuable information or reading material. However, no one expects teacher-librarians to watch the Disney Channel, MTV, or the latest blockbuster movies. It is not necessary to follow ESPN and/or the X Games with the ferocity of a fan. One need not listen to Top 20 countdowns, or follow underground music movements. Instead there are online shortcuts that will help you grow your repertoire of popular culture in an easy, and less time-consuming manner.

It has become easier, if at times overwhelming, to remain current. A strong PLN helps you cope with the latest educational theory (or fad), the changes in technology and the opportunities they create in our classrooms, the latest award-winning or popular literature, and the trends outside of school that impact our students learning experiences. A strong PLN can provide education and help teacher-librarians take advantage of trends, policies, and changes in the global community.

ADVOCACY

Another reason to build a strong PLN with a focus on professional development is advocacy. In the current U.S. public education system, advocacy is a large piece of the teacher-librarian's job responsibilities, even when it is not found in the actual job description. We must build partnerships with our community of staff, students, and parents. We work as educators to inform our administrators and school boards about the value of school library programs. We work with our state and national legislators to encourage governmental support for school libraries. If we do not engage in this important activity a crucial piece of student's learning experiences, the school library, may disappear. PLNs provide not only valuable support, but also fresh advocacy ideas. They prevent us from having to reinvent the wheel.

Beyond the support and fresh ideas, the community within your PLN can also function as advocates on your behalf. For example, when the news that Santa Rosa City Schools was posted by a distressed teacher-librarian looking for support on a California School Library Association (CSLA) listserv (CALib K–12), the response was immediate. CSLA members posted responses on an online input page developed by Santa Rosa City Schools regarding the proposed cuts; and, eventually, closing the libraries was tabled. Although not a complete victory, the virtual support was important in assisting the teacher-librarians in Santa Rosa to keep their school library doors open. Building a professional network is imperative in advocacy.

PLNs are instrumental in our professional growth, they alleviate the isolation, provide valuable support, open our schools to fresh ideas, strengthen our programs, and assist in developing our professional leadership. Fortunately, in the digital age developing that PLN is simple.

The next chapter investigates the tools that have been in place for a number of years that help us grow our learning networks, and provide professional development: conferences, listservs, online courses, and so on. Even these familiar events and tools have taken on new meanings and provide new opportunities in today's digital environment.

CHAPTER 3
Professional Development 1.0

Teacher-librarians are familiar with an "old-school" professional development option that I call Professional Development 1.0. For example, many school districts provide professional development meetings and seminars to the entire staff. Although we all have attended these required sessions, much of the time, school- or district-sponsored professional development sessions have not quite met our needs. Teacher-librarians have learned to search out professional development in conferences, listservs, and professional reading.

In order to continue learning and growing in our profession, many of us have established a PLN that involves meeting others at conferences or regional workshops, participating on listservs, and taking online classes. We understand the necessity of searching outside our content area to learn and make connections. We have developed relationships, both personal and professional, in which we may only see the other person once a year, or only know the person as a screen name or by his or her e-mail address; and we look forward to meeting at conferences so we can put a face to the name at the bottom of the e-mail or the screen name of the person with whom we have been chatting.

Some teacher-librarians have been active participants in Professional Development 1.0, presenting or posting frequently, others are content to "lurk," attending conferences, and reading the e-mails that came through daily. Each has value and each offers a unique learning opportunity. New tools discussed in this book do not devalue the old tools in building a learning network. Older tools are still valuable and user friendly. As such, when building your own learning network these tools should not be overlooked, and the manner in which they have evolved can maximize their impact. The next section evaluates the old 1.0 tools, their value, how they have changed, and how they can be used to increase one's learning opportunities.

FACE-TO-FACE LEARNING

Conferences are an excellent opportunity, not only to learn, but also to build personal relationships with other teacher-librarians. Teacher-librarians have an opportunity to attend sessions that may introduce new ideas for providing services to staff or learning opportunities for students. They can talk to vendors and seek new solutions to their library's needs. At formal events like dinners and lunches they can hear a keynote speaker, as well as meet new people at their table. They have an opportunity to share stories, discuss solutions, and commiserate or brag about their library, students, and staff. As an attendee of conferences, the feeling of isolation can be temporarily forgotten; it is reinvigorating to be surrounded by those who speak "your language."

Attending conferences is hardly a new idea, and it is one with which I expect readers are familiar. Now it is time to move to the front of the room. Teacher-librarians interested in truly expanding their horizons and improving conference experiences should consider presenting at a conference. Do not assume that because you know something, other teacher-librarians do so also. It may be that you have something surprising to contribute to the profession. Preparing a presentation for a conference can give you a deeper understanding of your topic. It will open up new information and avenues for exploration and evaluation. Presenting also offers you the opportunity to begin a discussion with other teacher-librarians who share your interest or passion for a specific topic. You can make surprising and interesting connections when opening up to a group of teacher-librarians who have their own experiences and thoughts on a topic. This can add unexpected depth to a conference experience. Furthermore, attendees may want to continue discussion after your presentation, which allows you to make new connections. Consider starting small, at a local or regional workshop, or even a state conference. Presenting provides a new outlook on conference attendance. Also consider that presenting may help defray costs, an issue for school libraries, particularly those located in more rural areas.

Finally, in-person attendance is only one way to benefit from a conference. In the virtual world, many conferences post handouts, podcasts, or videos of sessions. They may post conference blogs or wikis, or provide virtual sessions. From the comfort of your own home you can benefit from a number of different conference experiences, without losing time at your site, or spending money for attendance. This concept is explored in more detail in the section on virtual attendance.

LIBRARY CONFERENCES

Many state or regional library organizations offer conferences or workshops. Some conferences are exclusively directed to school libraries, and their staff, such as the CSLA's annual conference. Others are a combination of all libraries such as the Texas Library Association's annual conference. State or regional conferences have the benefit of being less costly, and in most cases easier to attend because of travel costs and arrangements. They have programs that relate directly to regional or state concerns, offering information on local legislative issues as well as general library and educational needs.

National and international conferences may also be of interest to teacher-librarians. Every two years AASL offers a national conference. The AASL conference makes an effort to reach all geographical areas of the contiguous United States by rotating the conference sites throughout the East, the South, the Midwest, and the West. Each year the American Library Association (ALA) holds a midwinter and an annual conference. The midwinter meeting is primarily committee, board, and council meetings; a time for the many volunteers to meet face-to-face and work on behalf of the organization. The annual ALA conference offers all-day preconferences, but it also offers general concurrent sessions that are two to four hours long throughout the conference as well as keynote speakers. The annual conference provides a greater opportunity for professional development. However, different divisions, including AASL, the Association of Library Services to Children (ALSC), and the Young Adult Library Services Association (YALSA) offer preconferences at the midwinter meetings in an effort to provide additional opportunities for learning.

The benefit of attending a conference with a diversity of library personnel is the ability to expand one's horizons beyond school libraries. Attending sessions sponsored by ALSC, YALSA, or the Public Library Association (PLA) may generate fresh ideas for your school library.

Library Conferences:

- *American Library Association (June)*
  - ○ http://www.ala.org : Select Events and Conferences link
- *American Association of School Libraries (Fall)*
  - ○ http://www.ala.org/ala/aasl/aaslindex.cfm
    AASL also hosts a page with links to affiliate's Web sites (often states). Search for information on Affiliate Assembly or related organizations. State Web sites will often contain information about local conferences and workshops.
- *International Association of School Libraries*
  - ○ http://www.iasl-online.org/
- *Public Library Association (Spring, Every 2 years)*
  - ○ http://www.placonference.org/

Occasionally, the youth divisions will sponsor joint sessions that encourage collaboration between school and public libraries. These suggestions have the potential to reduce a teacher-librarian's isolation upon return to a site because they encourage partnership with other librarians in the area. Teacher-librarians might also consider researching other division's conferences or workshops such as PLA or YALSA's Young Adult Literature Symposium, a new program that will be offered every two years.

An international library conference also occurs on an annual basis. The International Association of School Libraries (IASL) also holds an annual conference. Although cost will most definitely be a consideration, the sites are draws themselves. Past conferences have been held in Taipei, Lisbon, Hong Kong, and Berkeley, California. Again the sessions provide fresh ideas and there is a unique opportunity to connect with teacher-librarians from around the world.

BEYOND THE LIBRARY

Stakeholders

The school library has a number of different stakeholders and interests. It is necessary to reach out beyond the library world in order to know what is current and interesting in other areas and to identify areas of collaboration. Each subject area similar to libraries will hold annual conferences, often both national and regional. For example, the National Council of Teachers of English (NCTE) holds a national conference in November, which includes a workshop by the Assembly of Literature for Adolescents (ALAN), while the National Science Teacher Association (NSTA) holds more regional events throughout the calendar year. Teacher-librarians who work closely with their English department or with reading specialists may want to consider attending the NCTE conference, especially if you can attend as collaborating partners. If you collaborate with social science, science, or other departments, they may want to consider attending the appropriate conference as a team with the teachers you work with. Investigation may lead to state conferences for subject areas in which you may not only attend, but also may consider presenting, particularly in a collaborative team.

Another avenue to explore in terms of school library stakeholders are the administrators with whom we work. The Association for Supervision and Curriculum Development (ASCD) offers several conferences throughout the year. Consider exploring the conference information on the ASCD Web site to understand the interests and the pressures facing school administrators. Perhaps you can find a solution to a concern; at the very least you may develop the language to discuss school libraries with your administrator. Other stakeholder organizations include the National School Board Association, and the Parent Teacher Association.

Related Organizations:

Core Subject Areas

- NCTE: English (November)
  http://www.ncte.org/profdev/conv/annual
- NSTA : Science (March)
  http://www.nsta.org/conferences/
- NCTM: Math (April)
  http://www.nctm.org/meetings/
- NCSS: Social Studies (November)
  http://www.ncss.org/conference/

Related Teacher Conferences

- National Middle School Association (November)
  http://www.nmsa.org/annual/

- International Reading Association
  http://www.reading.org/association/meetings/annual.html
  IRA also hosts links to regional meetings and conferences on its Web site.
- International Society of Technology Educators (June)
  http://www.iste.org/(NECC link)
- ASCD (April)
  http://www.ascd.org/portal/site/ascd
- PTA (June)
  http://www.pta.org/

Related Organizations

Closely related organizations are other avenues to explore. For example, the International Reading Association (IRA) and ISTE both sponsor annual conferences. The IRA offers different conferences including a national convention (held in the United States or Canada), a research conference, and a world congress held in international cities. ISTE holds a national convention called the National Education Computing Conference (NECC). Within ISTE is the Special Interest Group for teacher-librarians (SIGMS). At NECC, SIGMS identifies sessions presented by members, as well as sessions of interest to "media specialists." Literacy and technology are two of the many hats teacher-librarians wear every day and interacting with other educators in these arenas is essential to our role, strengthening our understandings and allowing us the opportunity to educate and advocate for our programs in these worlds.

VIRTUAL ATTENDANCE

Although the ability to physically attend a conference is preferable, it can be difficult for teacher-librarians. It may only be possible financially and physically to attend local conferences; or one may be able to leave one's site once a year. Although some conferences are held during the summer months, many do take place during the school year. It is often necessary to make a choice regarding which conference to attend. For example, the ALA annual conference and NECC often occur at the same or similar times. In the 21st Century actual attendance is not necessary to gain valuable information from a variety of conferences. Figure 1.1 graphically represented my attendance at NECC as a virtual attendee. So what does that look like?

The first step in exploring a conference without attending is to peruse the conference Web site. What sessions and keynote speakers are included? What information can be gleaned from the conference program? For example, in June 2008, ASCD offered a summer conference that included a strand on differentiated instruction. Ask yourself whether the library can participate in differentiated instruction. Do you know what it is? What can you learn?

Merely investigating conference programs can give you an area to research and explore on your own. In fact, you may often explore concepts within the convention's Web site. Increasingly organizations are posting handouts from sessions online. These only may be available for a short time so you should check in shortly after the conference is concluded. Although reading the handouts may not give you the complete session experience, it is an excellent place to begin.

Helpful Hint: Explore the conference Web site for free resources

---

In some instances, organizations will also post podcasts (download-able audio) or video of sessions. An organization that truly provides a potential virtual learning experience is ISTE's NECC Web site. This Web site posts handouts, podcasts, and video, as well as archives the sessions. The benefit of archives is the ability to access information in a just-in-time manner—when you are ready for it. NECC also links sessions to blog posts about sessions. Spending a few moments exploring a conference Web site may reveal a number of tools to access the conference without the cost of attending, and provide the ability to learn on your own time.

Blogs are another way to "virtually attend" a conference. Many attendees will "live blog" sessions, posting their notes for their readers. Others will post responses after the session. Searching for a blog tag on Technorati or Google blog search will reveal a number of posts about conferences.

Blog Search Engines

- Technorati
  http://technorati.com/
- Google
  http://blogsearch.google.com/
- Ice Rocket
  http://www.icerocket.com/

Other organizations or conference presenters will post conference wikis that will encourage interaction. The links to wikis will be present in conference handouts or on the Web sites. The interactive nature of wikis may provide an opportunity to learn beyond the session information from a larger number of people. The difficulty of learning solely from blogs and wikis is that often you are only reading someone else's perspective. What the person "live blogging" or creating a wiki feels important enough to record may not speak to you. Without hearing the presentation, you may miss a piece that was important to you and your site. Blogs and wikis are best when used to supplement a podcast or video of a complete presentation.

If you are interested in virtual attendance. Hitchhikr (http://hitchhikr.com/wordpress/) is a conference aggregator designed by David Warlick. It uses common tags to collect blog entries, podcasts, and Flickr photos connected to a single conference. Conferences are listed by date and are available in one space, making it an excellent tool for those interested in what is happening at conferences that they are unable to attend. The listed conferences are primarily ed-tech and technology conferences but the information is easily accessible by anyone. Overall, there is opportunity in virtual attendance of face-to-face conferences that is worth exploring.

ONLINE COURSES

In the process of meeting the formal requirements set forth by school districts, state mandates, or your personal wishes, one opportunity is to take online courses. Teacher-librarians have a choice of several different types of online courses. The most traditional online courses offer an opportunity for guided learning with deadlines and check-in dates. More organizations and businesses are offering courses that are self-paced, with the onus entirely on the individual to complete the course. These are provided in several delivery formats.

In some cases, online learning is constructed in traditional course format using course management tools such as Moodle, allowing for posted readings, comments, posting papers and responses, and even online quizzes. Other courses are nothing more than lectures, accessible via video. Webcasts and webinars take the video lecture format one step further by providing the opportunity for interaction. Using a variety of tools, participants can ask questions or discuss a lecture.

Of course, virtual courses have their pros and cons. The benefit of learning via online courses is the ability to learn at your own pace at a convenient time. The drawback is that it requires self-motivation. Still, a structured course may be the only motivation that you need, and if you tried it once and didn't like, you will now find the delivery tools are improving, as are the courses themselves. Since the popularization of the Internet, universities and professional development organizations have worked to improve virtual education and online learning. They offer an ever-widening range of opportunities. One can work to achieve a master's degree online, take continuing education units, or merely participate in courses that are interesting, relevant, and further the professional knowledge of an individual.

There is usually a cost associated with most online courses; however there are a few structured learning opportunities that are free. Furthermore, there are archived opportunities that are free. The experience may not be as rich as participating face-to-face while the course or webinar is taking place, but it does provide immediate access at a convenient and relevant time.

Organizations and Other Agencies

One of the benefits of membership in an organization is access to on-line professional development at a reduced rate. The national divisions of the ALA, ALSC, AASL, and YALSA offer online professional development to anyone who registers; however these courses are offered at a reduced rate to members. ALSC uses Moodle to provide guided learning in issues related to children librarianship. AASL offers both self-paced and facilitated learning opportunities. YALSA's professional development courses are facilitated, and are the equivalent of a one-day face-to-face workshop.

A national agency offering continuing education opportunities is the Library of Congress. The Library of Congress provides sessions for both large groups and individuals through its American Memory collection (http://memory.loc.gov/learn/educators/workshop/ssindex.html). The self-serve courses are primarily designed for use in a history curriculum, but instruction on using primary sources, and the technology components should be of interest to teacher-librarians. Using the American Memory collection to collaborate with social science teachers is an excellent opportunity for building relationships within your site with other teachers as you demonstrate this level of expertise and illustrate your leadership capacity. Remember, although there are many opportunities for library professionals, the prospects for K–12 teachers should be explored as they offer an excellent opening for developing leadership skills, collaborative partnerships, and advocacy for your school library program, as well as strengthening one's understanding and comfort in the curricular areas of a school.

State and regional library institutions and organizations may also offer online courses, or may partner with universities and businesses to provide online course material. An example of an institution offering courses is InfoPeople, a grant-funded program that provides training in conjunction with the California State Library. InfoPeople provides training both in a face-to-face environment and online. Face-to-face training is only available in California, but the online training sessions are available to anyone in the United States. InfoPeople sessions have a cost associated with their sessions, which are both online courses and webcasts. InfoPeople does provide access to archived webcasts that are available for free and to anyone in the world.

Another example would be the state library of Texas, which also includes professional development in an online learning format. The state of Washington offers online, self-guided learning opportunities. Idaho offers online training for untrained librarians, including a program that focuses on youth services. Idaho's training program may at first appear too basic to assist teacher-librarians, but it may be helpful for paraprofessionals to participate, or as a refresher for teacher-librarians. As with the InfoPeople program, these programs are directed to the needs of the state (hence Idaho's program for working librarians with no university-level training), however, contacting the organization about participation is always a possibility. In fact, most state libraries offer some professional development so it is recommended that you investigate your state library to learn about the opportunities.

Library organizations may offer the most relevant professional development that is focused on the needs of school and public librarians who work with youth. Professional development in library-related fields develops a common academic knowledge and vocabulary. But it is important to consider expanding beyond the library world, to build partnerships across the curriculum of schools. Teacher-librarians may wish to join and use the opportunities offered by educational organizations such as the ISTE.

At the national level, ISTE offers a number of online professional development opportunities in the ed-tech arena at a cost. Ongoing webinars cover a variety of topics; and, although they are available to anyone interested, ISTE offers a reduced rate for its members. Webinars take place at a specific time, and feature a presenter, but also offer an opportunity for interaction. Information on ISTE's webinars can be found on the ISTE Web site (http://www.iste.org) on the Educator's Resources page by clicking on the "Professional Development" link. Generally, they include the use of both your computer and your telephone. ISTE also offers a page that links to a number of other professional development opportunities. You can find the page under Educator Resources > Training on the ISTE Web page. In many ways ISTE is an excellent partner organization to ALA, with its focus on ed-tech, a special interest group for teacher-librarians, and National Educational Technology Standards (NETS) that complement AASL's student learning standards.

Universities

Universities have been in the lead in providing online curriculum. Most universities offer some level of continuing education (CE) credits, several of which are solely virtual. CE programs in a virtual environment are especially important for teacher-librarians who are isolated from higher education for geographical reasons. School librarians who do not already hold a master's degree may be interested in earning the degree, which often pays for itself in increased salary.

Many universities offer online master's programs, although many combine face-to-face instruction with virtual education. Virtual learning has its drawbacks and these should be considered in pursuing this option; it is difficult to embrace a class' enthusiasm for a topic, the opportunity to learn from your peers by serendipitous conversation is limited, and self-motivation is essential. For most teacher-librarians CE credits are preferable. One example is San Jose State University's partnership with Neal-Schuman Professional Education Network to offer CE credit in courses such as Searching 2.0 and Meeting the Needs of At Risk Readers. Simmons College also offers online workshops such as Digital Imaging and Instructional Design: Creating Materials for an Online Course.

The University of Wisconsin Madison also offers virtual CE, including traditional courses such as collection development, as well as courses that explore new trends such as "Gaming as Service" offered in fall 2008. The University of Maryland provides an online interactive tutorial on copyright issues and concerns. Indiana University and the Institute of Museum and Library services offer an online course in outcome-based planning and evaluation. A little research can provide information on different university programs in a short amount of time.

Do not limit yourself to considering only online courses in library and information science. Teachers have many opportunities, too. It would be difficult to outline all of the many university and professional development programs. Again, it will take very little research to identify courses that may be beneficial to a teacher-librarian.

Companies

Many companies that provide services to school libraries also offer professional development. Often, one must be a patron of the business before they will provide information regarding their training. This includes automation solutions, digital media, and databases; however, some companies provide free access to ongoing professional development. The SirsiDynix Institute (http://www.sirsidynixinstitute.com/) allows free access to speakers and events. Using LiveMeeting, participants can register for free web conferences. They archive past seminars so you may access just-in-time instruction.

Free Online Courses

One staff development program, 23 Things, explores new Web 2.0 tools. This program has been adapted in a number of ways, allowing individuals to participate and learn for free. The 23 Things program was developed by Helen Blowers of the Public Library of Charlotte & Mecklenburg County with support and assistance from her staff.

---

23 Things Programs

- The Original
  http://plcmcl2-about.blogspot.com/
- CSLA
  http://schoollibrarylearning2.blogspot.com/
- InfoPeople
  http://our23things.infopeople.org/
- School Library Journal
  http://www.schoollibraryjournal.com/blog/290000629.html
- Woodward Academy
  http://k12learning20.wikispaces.com/

Blowers credits basing the program loosely on "Stephen Abram's article, 43 Things I (or You) might want to do this year (Information Outlook - Feb 2006) and the website 43Things" (http://plcmcl2-about.blogspot.com/). The original staff development program has encouraged other organizations to develop their own projects including CSLA.

CSLA developed "School Library Learning 2.0" in summer 2007 which focuses on school libraries. In summer 2008, the *School Library Journal* (*SLJ*) offered a "23 things" course through its Web site hosted by Michael Stephens. The number of 23 Things programs being offered to K–12 teachers or library workers is increasing as more state organizations design programs for their members. The approach to a 23 Things learning program is self-paced but "coaches" are provided to answer questions. Within each program, there often are cohort groups, allowing a number of people to learn together as well as to share ideas. For example, individuals participating in *SLJ*'s training can share with one another, and those participating in CSLA's program can share with other participants of CSLA's training. The variety of courses from different organizations share a similar aspect in that 23 Things is a unique blend of online learning that is both self-paced and collaborative. It is primarily an individual experience designed to introduce teacher-librarians to social networking tools, while participating cohort groups network and learn together.

---

23 Things You Might Learn

1. Blog applications
2. Avatar generators
3. Wikis
4. Photosharing applications such as Flickr
5. RSS and news readers such as Bloglines or Google Reader
6. Custom search engines such as Rollyo
7. Image generators such as Image Chef
8. Social bookmarking such as Del.icio.us or Diigo
9. Blog search engines such as Technorati
10. Video-sharing sites such as YouTube
11. Social networking sites for particular items such as Library Thing
12. Searching for and creating podcasts

13. Audio books and E-books

14. Online communities such as Ning or Facebook

15. Online tools: word processing, etc.

16. Copyright and creative commons

17. Online media albums such as Voicethread

18. Image capture and sharing such as Jing

19. Searching video or television with a service such as Blinxx

20. Setting up an iGoogle page

21. Creating video set to music with a service such as Animoto

22. Exploring online collaboration services such as Gliffy, or Google Docs

23. Online organizational tools such as Remember the Milk

Have fun !!!!

WebJunction (http://www.webjunction.org/) is a mixture of free and paid online learning opportunities for libraries. Funded by the Bill and Melinda Gates Foundation and housed within the Online Computer Library Center (OCLC), WebJunction is a growing community of libraries and librarians. The online seminars are primarily from University of North Texas' Project Le@d program, which is also connected to AASL professional development. Although concurrent participation has a nominal cost ($20), the archived programs may be accessed for free. A variety of tools and resources are available on WebJunction, which will assist any librarian in professional growth. This is explored in the next chapter.

Another free resource to explore is Apple's iTunes U. iTunes U places content on iTunes that is available for download from educational institutions that span the globe. Primarily, the content is podcasts, but there are also videos and lesson plans. Content providers include Stanford University, Yale, the Smithsonian, and various smaller institutions. Also included is international subject matter from other countries such as Australia, New Zealand, Ireland, and England. State departments of education and K–12 institutions also provide video and podcasts. Content is divided by subject and includes teaching and learning, as well as K–12 core subject areas (English, math, social science, and science). It is possible to download a video or a podcast on a portable media player such as an iPod and take your learning on the go.

The benefit of portable learning is obvious, and the price is right. It is possible to search for a lecture or content that highlights a particular interest. The flaw of iTunes U is that it lacks interaction. Although you may learn something, you will have not formed new partnerships, or friendships, nor had the opportunity to interact with an expert by asking questions or debating a point. Still iTunes U can fill a niche.

Although online learning is nothing new, Web 2.0 tools improve access, as well as the ability to interact. Furthermore, the number of free resources that can be accessed has increased, particularly in archived material. The main benefit of archived video and webcasts is that it is "just-in-time learning." The ability to search archives and videos to fulfill an immediate information need is one of the benefits of the digital age.

LISTSERVS

Listservs, in and among themselves, are not true professional development tools, but they are excellent vehicles for expanding one's professional knowledge. Listservs have been common in the library profession for at least the past 10 years. They are a free service that is delivered to the desktop frequently (perhaps too frequently). Using e-mail, a list can bring together those with common interests to share knowledge, gain support, and reinforce the ideals of a profession. The knowledge on a listserv is generally collective knowledge, complete with misinformation, opinions, and valuable insights. Using the threaded discussions on a listserv will help you keep current in a particular field (especially in the area of literature); however, readers may find that some conversations appear recycled. Discussions also provide suggestions for avenues of deeper research and understanding, and perhaps most importantly grant a sense of connection with others who share your passions. In general listservs are an excellent daily tool, if managed correctly. **Do not be afraid to delete!**

Lm_Net: The Standard

The most familiar, and perhaps the largest list is LM_Net. LM_Net, which will be in its mid-teens by 2009, currently boasts more than 16,000 subscribers. LM_Net traffics 100 messages per day on average. The collective brain can answer questions, inspire fields of inquiry, explore common and/or current debates, frustrate, or infuriate. Often, teacher-librarians, and other library workers, will comment on their ability to amaze others with a quick answer to a difficult question in their requests for information from the collective whole. Debates can seem tedious after a time, with little new insight, but the initial posts can provide food for thought. LM_Net is a moderated listserv; the moderators reserve the right to end a "thread" based on the rules established when you subscribe. Even as a moderated list, the high volume requires e-mail management skills such as a second e-mail address or e-mail folders. It requires the ability to delete and move on; but it also provides easy access to thousands of school and public librarians, as well as friends of school libraries such as ed-tech gurus and the vendors who monitor the list traffic.

Visit http://www.eduref.org/lm_net/ to subscribe to Lm_Net

Literature Listservs

Another well-established, and frequently visited list is Child_Lit. Also well into its teens and boasting a large volume of messages per day, Child_lit is an unmoderated list "convened for the express purpose of examining the theory and criticism of literature for children and young adults" (https://mailman.rutgers.edu/mailman/listinfo/child_lit). If you are searching for in-depth discussions that are often theory-based, with a healthy dose of disagreement Child_Lit is an excellent list. Similar to LM_Net the volume can be difficult to manage.

Visit http://www.rci.rutgers.edu/~mjoseph/childlit/about.html to subscribe to Child_Lit.

Another group dedicated to the discussion of books is AdBooks, a Yahoo group focusing on books for teens. AdBooks sponsors an "online book club." The AdBooks discussions can range from in-depth analysis, to recommendations, to the JHUNT awards, which are decided annually by list members. AdBooks may be a more manageable list for middle-grade and high school teacher-librarians.

AdBooks

Visit http://www.adbooks.org/ to join AdBooks

Organizational Listservs

Other lists include those sponsored by organizations. AASLForum allows school librarians to discuss school library related issues, as well as AASL-related issues and news. INFOLIT is operated with the ACRL, and is for the sharing of ideas on teaching information literacy skills. For those interested in AASL, and the work of the organization, AASLNews is a small traffic listserv that provides timely information.

Visit http://www.ala.org/ala/aasl/aaslproftools/aaslprofessional.cfm to subscribe to AASL's lists

YALSA also has listservs that are of interest to school librarians. YALSA-BK is a high-traffic listserv (50 to 75 messages per day) that discusses current YA literature. Smaller lists sponsored by YALSA include YA Music, and YA_YAAC for programming ideas and encouraging youth involvement.

Visit http://www.ala.org/ala/yalsa/electronicresourcesb/ electronicresources.cfm for YALSA's lists.

Managing lists can be time-consuming and one must carefully consider the value of subscribing to any one list. How does it help you improve your program, make you a better teacher, or provide service to your patrons? What is the value of time spent? Still, as an "old-school" tool, information is delivered to you; and it provides access to thousands of people who share your interests and concerns on a global basis. If you are willing to participate, you, too, can provide just-in-time answers to pressing questions.

ACTIVE PARTICIPATION IN ORGANIZATIONS

One of the best options to help acquire leadership skills is to participate in organizations whose mission is to support school libraries, student learning, and integration of skills into student's core curriculum. Organizations have a need for volunteers in order to complete the work of the organization, including training, lobbying, standards building, and collaboration with other educational organizations. Members of many organizations are actively working to help their organizations become more flexible entities that can respond to members' needs in a timely manner. Volunteering within an organization is an excellent way to immerse yourself in your profession and to learn skills as well as information that will translate in your school environment.

It is easy to get involved in an organization, and the possibility of it being free to the volunteer also exists. Professional organizations often suffer a lack of volunteers, and as a result they tend to rely on the same people. Volunteers who bring a fresh perspective are eagerly accepted. If you are concerned about time commitments, consider volunteering to serve on a task force, or something similar, which has a limited time frame and a specific task. If travel and cost is a concern, research the reimbursement policies or focus on local organizations. Another option is to consider serving as a virtual committee member.

Many school librarians in rural areas find themselves isolated, with the cost and distance of travel making active participation difficult if not impossible. However, increasing numbers of organizations are offering the possibility of participating virtually. Although conference attendance is one way to maximize your membership, you should consider finding a way to volunteer in the leadership or work of an organization virtually.

This chapter has covered professional development from a more traditional approach. The next chapter introduces school librarians to Professional Development 2.0.

CHAPTER 4
Professional Development 2.0

As the Internet has evolved and tools have become both free and user friendly, the opportunity for professional development and the ability to make connections has greatly improved. The new landscape provides unique opportunities to learn, and perhaps most important for isolated teacher-librarians, it provides the ability to make global connections with other teacher-librarians. We can share, brag, commiserate, and support.

You may be thinking that we do that on LM_Net and have done so for many years, and you would not be wrong. The new tools supplement the already vibrant school library learning community. In some cases a newer 2.0 tool may be a preferred tool. In others the tools succeed beyond e-mail in building communities and making connections. In still others the opportunity to share is immensely improved. Many Web 2.0 tools are designed to improve your experiences, provide tools for collaboration, and offer simple online publishing applications.

In the following pages, I examine wikis, blogs, social bookmarking, social networking, podcasting, vodcasting, and short message blogging as ways to expand your PLN and provide professional development. You may want to explore the wide variety of applications beyond what is focused on in this book, for example, online time management (calendars, to-do lists) or online image editing (Flickr or Animoto). The sites recommended in the following box are aggregators of different applications, and may lead you to a new tool to add to your toolbox.

Web 2.0 Application Searches

Go2Web20
  http://www.go2web20.net/
Feed My App
  http://www.feedmyapp.com
Kathy Schrock's Bookmarks
  http://www.diigo.com/list/Kathyschrock/web20tools
CloudTrip
  http://www.cloudtrip.com/

Professional Development 2.0 does not ignore the tools we have always used. Rather it enhances conferences, online courses, and learning, and provides texture to the communities that exist. In some ways, it is disingenuous to separate the two learning experiences into the old and the new. As discussed in the previous chapter, many of the newer tools are used to enhance the many ways we already learn. In this chapter, as well as in the next, I explore the Web 2.0 tools: RSS feeds, wikis, and blogs. In subsequent chapters, I focus on the social networking tools, including social bookmarking, the audiovisual components of podcasting and online video, and information-management tools such as personal home pages, as well as the concept of "unplugging."

RSS FEEDS: THE BEGINNING

One of the best tools for organizing daily information is an RSS feed aggregator. What is RSS feed? RSS stands for Real Simple Syndication and there is a technical explanation for RSS and how it works. What is most important, in simple language, is that RSS feed allows you to obtain updates of blogs, podcasts, and news feeds. In the Web 2.0 environment most pages have an RSS feed that will allow users to aggregate information in one place. Pages that offer a subscription to RSS will often host the symbol below either on their page or in the URL bar at the top of the page.

In order to maximize RSS, one should set up an aggregator such as Bloglines or Google Reader. In one convenient place, a user can manage updates to pages visited regularly. It is a fairly easy matter if the page has an RSS feed.

Aggregators

The members of your PLN can be gathered in one place; most of your network will host blogs, wikis, or be active participants on Nings or other social networking sites. Like all day-to-day management systems, when using an aggregator it will be important to be able to sift through information to identify what deserves more time, and what you may quickly pass over. As we spend more time examining the new Web 2.0 applications and how they can assist in developing a PLN that focuses on professional growth, developing a healthy aggregator will be a fundamental need.

Bloglines and Google Reader are the most popular services. The sidebar delivers instructions for setting up a Bloglines account, but it is not an endorsement over Google Reader. Each reader offers the opportunity to subscribe to personal feeds, organize feeds by folders, search for new feeds, and share with friends. Bloglines allows you to clip and save blog entries, as well as create your own blog. Find the reader that works for you.

Bloglines

Setting Up a Bloglines Account

1. You will find the link to **register** in the upper right corner of the page in small print.
2. After receiving the confirmation e-mail, use the subscribe window through the e-mail link.
3. You have two subscription options to get you started: Quick Picks and Popular Subscriptions. Feel free to ignore or use them as trial feeds.
4. To develop personal feeds click on the link (again small text) for an **Easy Subscribe Button**
   a. Each browser will have different instructions for the button, which is a necessity for making Bloglines easy to use.

WIKIS

Wikis are perhaps the most familiar and well used of Web 2.0 applications; the "killer app" for many teacher-librarians. A wiki is a simple

Web page that anyone can add content to and edit, using basic word-processing tools and very simple techniques that allow for hyperlinking, and image and video insertions. Several software applications are available that allow users to create wikis and these can be private or public. Because of their ease of use, wikis, like blogs, open the world of Web site creation to anyone with a computer and Internet access. Wikis are more reminiscent of static Web pages. They are not static, however, because of the ability of a number of users to edit the pages. They can be used to collect links and index information, plan across distances and in asynchronous time, write collaboratively and/or create a Web presence. Wikis are an essential tool and familiarity is a necessity.

Wikis: Collaborative Professional Development

To maximize your experience engaging in a wiki, it is better to be a content producer and a user. However, learning is still taking place without being an active participant. Because of the collaborative nature of wikis, they are an excellent place to collect examples of effective practice, share lesson plans, and provide links to online resources for reading and core subject areas. Some wikis showcase newer ed-tech tools, and effective integration into classroom instruction. You will find that many wikis grow out of, or are precursors to presentations, and they allow attendees and other visitors to collaborate and "grow" the information of a presentation. An excellent place to get started with wikis, are those connected to conferences.

As teacher-librarians, often working alone in a school, wikis are a *tool* that allows collaboration. Although they are excellent planning tools, wikis are not necessarily conversational tools (a forum on a Ning, addressed later, would be a preferred application). However, because of the ability to be user-generated, indexes on wikis are particularly helpful in locating a wide variety of sites and information. An example would be Donna Baumbach's and Judy Lee's WebTools4U2Use. (http://webtools4u2use.wikispaces.com/) This wiki also includes examples of how other teacher-librarians have used the tools, which can be an excellent way to encourage oneself to try something new, investigate a different assignment, or generate a fresh approach to an old topic. As a starting place, WebTools4U2Use is an excellent site that will introduce you to a number of tools, and begin your journey of connections.

Wikis are an easy place to share best practices. You can attach documents to wikis, which make them easy places to upload lesson plans, or handouts. Library Success (http://www.libsuccess.org/) is a large wiki designed for this purpose. Its focus is public libraries, but there is relevant and important information for teacher-librarians as well.

Active Participation

Wikis as collaborative spaces harness the most professional development power when they are open and encourage participation. Wikipedia would be a large-scale example of an open, editable, discussable information space. As an example, it also illustrates the concern with open space, in the ability of the information to be "vandalized," or replaced with inaccurate data. Although the response to vandals by users on Wikipedia and other wikis is often swift, some wiki creators choose to protect their wikis by asking that you register in order to edit pages, or by "locking" pages to anonymous edits. Registration is free, takes little time, and allows you to "meet" other information consumer and creators with your interests.

Library Success is an example of a wiki that has struggled with vandals and has chosen this route. It is still worth the time to register. Web 2.0 is built on the concept of information creation and sharing among a global community. Actively participating in the communities surrounding the tools that you use will help you become an integral part of the global ed-tech and school library community.

Evaluating Examples

One of the best things you can do to bring a fresh perspective to your library program is to peruse the examples of how teachers are using wikis. This will generate ideas for your own program and your own personal wiki. Wikis can be used for professional portfolios, and digital storage spaces on a personal professional level. They can be used with classes to build common knowledge, share new information, and practice writing for an audience with peer review. Wikis are an essential component of a PLN, a site that leads one to new ideas, and new tools. They may also lead you to trusted collaborators and experts in a field.

As a professional development tool, wikis serve two purposes. The first is that learning how to use a wiki is an essential component to today's technology. Wikis have multiple uses in classrooms, school libraries, and professional purposes. The second is that wiki sites have become valuable resources for new ideas via examples and indexes.

Recommended Wikis

Professional Development Wikis

Organizations
ISTE Wiki (http://www.iste.wikispaces.net/): Although membership makes the ISTE wiki more useful, there are still plenty of free resources to be found, and discussions to investigate.

YALSA Wiki (http://wikis.ala.org/yalsa/index.php/Main_Page): The YALSA wiki includes information on the organization, advocacy, programming, technology, literature, and youth participation.

ALSC Wiki (http://wikis.ala.org/alsc/index.php/Main_Page): The ALSC wiki contains information and resources on the organization including selection committees, resources including software reviews, and technology ideas.

MIT Open Courseware (http://ocw.mit.edu/OcwWeb/web/home/home/index.htm): This wiki offers access to the course syllabus, materials, lecture notes, and so on, from MIT classes.

Individual/Group Wikis
Curriki (http://www.curriki.org/): Advertised as Wikipedia for curriculum, Curriki has grown into a wiki hosting more than 17,000 resources including lesson plans that are reviewed by its more than 40,000 members, and the ability to connect with teachers from diverse geographical backgrounds to collaborate on units of instruction and classroom projects.

OER Commons (http://www.oercommons.org/): Open Educational Resources provides lesson plans, learning modules, resources, and assessment items. Similar to Curriki, there are materials for primary, secondary, and postsecondary educators.

Wiki Educator (http://www.wikieducator.org/Main_Page): This is another wiki whose goal is to provide collaborative space for educators to plan projects together and develop free content.

Educational Wikis (http://educationalwikis.wikispaces.com/): This wiki provides resources for learning how to use wikis, examples of wikis used in the K–12 environment, and a collaborative space for sharing ideas.

WebTools4You2Use   (http://webtools4u2use.wikispaces.com/): Conceived by Bambach and Lee of University of Central Florida, this wiki will help expand your horizons using Web 2.0 social media tools. There are numerous resources, including links to examples of how the various tools are used. You can spend hours learning from the resources on this wiki, which as a collaborative environment encourages participation.

Ambient Librarian (http://www.ambientlibrarian.org/): This is similar to a 23 Things blog course in that it explores Web 2.0 tools for use in library services. There are also fabulous examples and numerous listed resources.

Library Success: A Best Practices Wiki (http://www.libsuccess.org/): A large wiki with a focus on public library services, there are still plenty of resources for teacher-librarians. This is a collaborative community in which members post success stories and identify resources.

Classroom 2.0 Wiki (http://www.classroom20wiki.com/): This wiki is designed to provide resources and professional development to teachers using Web 2.0 tools in their classrooms.

Advocates for Digital Citizenship, Safety, and Success (http://ad4dcss. wikispaces.com/): This global community advocates for digital citizenship, responsible behavior in the digital world, and the education of people on digital citizenship. As a growing wiki, it still needs collaborative input but it is ambitious in scope and does provide resources and ideas in teaching digital citizens.

David Warlick's Co-Learners (http://davidwarlick.com/wiki/pmwiki. php/Main/HomePage): This is an extensive wiki that supports David Warlick's presentations with access to resources, readings, podcasting, and so on. Warlick spends considerable time exploring the notion of PLNs, and it is worth a visit to the suite of sites he maintains (blog, wiki, Web site, etc.) to explore PLNs in greater depth.

Digital Bookends (http://digitalbookends.pbwiki.com/): A wide variety of resources are found here for teacher-librarians including book reviews, Web 2.0 tools, instructional and parent Web sites, as well as other pages of interest to those working in school libraries.

Connectivity (http://www.connectivism.ca/): George Siemens hosts this wiki, which examines learning theories of new digital literacy and social networking. This is an excellent wiki to visit and participate in if you are interested in the theory behind using Web 2.0 tools with students.

Information Fluency (http://informationfluency.wikispaces.com/): The list of resources and examples on this site are impressive. It also includes links to Joyce Valenza's (the host) presentations. If you are looking for new educational tools, this wiki is an excellent resource.

Educational Origami (http://edorigami.wikispaces.com/): This wiki connects information and communications technologies to Bloom's taxonomies and discusses integration of educational technology into curriculum.

Books and Reading Wikis
Book Lust (http://booklust.wetpaint.com/): This is a community dedicated to books and reading, and yes, it is connected to Nancy Pearl. She has information regarding her books and appearances but more important there is a community of readers sharing recommendations for books, book clubs, and reader's advisory, as well as active discussion on book topics taking place.

Child Lit Wiki (http://childlit.info/): This site includes a collection of reviews, articles, recommendations, and lists for children's literature. The site can be browsed by topic and theme, an organization that is particularly helpful to teacher-librarians. It also is an open community soliciting expertise from the community of children's literature, teachers, librarians, authors, and so on.

Teen Lib Wiki (http://yalibrarian.com/yalib_wiki/): Hosted by the Alternative Teen Services site, this wiki contains pages and articles relating to YA literature, programming, crafts, and general resources. If you work with tweens and/or teens, this is an excellent place to visit and collaborate with other adolescent advocates.

Library Goddesses Wiki (http://librarygoddesses.pbwiki.com/): Primarily focused on literature (although there are programming resources as well), this wiki seeks active collaboration in building a home for the collection of booklists based on theme, age, best of . . . , and the wide variety of book lists for children and teens that we all create.

Booklists (http://booklists.wikispaces.com/): Another booklist wiki, this one is directed to adults and young adults and is arranged primarily by theme.

Wikibooks (http://en.wikibooks.org/wiki/WB:FB): This is a collection of online textbooks including *WikiJunior*, which is designed for children, and *Simple English*.

Example Wikis
Flat Classroom Project (http://flatclassroomproject.wikispaces.com/): Flat Classroom is designed to build a collaborative classroom for global school community. Resources include lesson plans for teachers as well as for students. It also links to the Horizon project (http://horizonproject.wikispaces.com/), which is the follow-up project to Flat Classroom.

Welkers Economics Wiki (http://welkerswikinomics.wetpaint.com/): A very impressive "experiment," this wiki is designed for advanced placement and international baccalaureate economics students, providing resources and collaborative learning space. This wiki was winner of the 2007 Edublog award.

AP Physics Assignment (http://hildeap.wetpaint.com/): This is an end-of-the-year assignment in which the students used WetPaint wikis to build "pseudoscience Web sites," giving the teachers opportunities to discuss Web evaluation and copyright issues. Representative student examples can be found at http://hydrationnation.wetpaint.com/ in which a student builds an alternative fuel argument using human urine, and http://jupitereffect.wetpaint.com/, which examines the Jupiter Effect. While the student examples are representative, it is a first year assignment that needs both instructional and assessment improvement.

BLOGS AND BLOGGING

When blogs first appeared they tended to be personal, online journals of day-to-day activities. Blogs have evolved beyond personal journals; and interactive Web sites that allow for comment and conversation are more common than static Web sites, and have aided the changing Web climate. Blogs have found a place in professional literature, as well as mainstream media. Experts, and your average Joe, use blogs to explore professional topics, new ideas, and common controversies. On popular blogs, the daily conversation through comments only enhances the initial post, although comments can also expose the problems of interactive media. Even the daily newspaper allows for commenting, in a more interactive exploration of a story.

The Pros and the Cons

In terms of daily professional development, blogs are similar to having professional journals at your fingertips. The benefit of reading blogs, in addition to the day-to-day nature, lies in both length of the initial post and the conversation that can occur. A number of professionals blog on a regular basis on a wide variety of topics, including libraries, information literacy, ed-tech concerns, professional reading, and literature. Developing "go-to" blogs that pique your interest, challenge your philosophies, and provide you with information is an essential component of building a PLN.

Blogs are not without their drawbacks. Unlike professional journals, there is no obvious vetting of information. Although persons who comment are quick to point out flaws and/or mistakes, the reader runs the risk of encountering false information or rumor, as evidenced by the large number of partisan blogs circulating rumors and misinformation. As information professionals, teacher-librarians are keenly aware of this concern. Furthermore, like all information, blog entries are filtered through the lens of the writer. Although some bloggers encourage the identification of biases upfront and permanently, this does not happen often. Comments, while having the benefit of extending the conversation, also run the risk of being attacked by trolls, people who deliberately create conflict. Although blogs have disadvantages, by considering these concerns you can find blogs that meet your needs and have professional credibility.

In the library blog community certain blogs and bloggers are more familiar and more popular than others. Similar to listservs, the interaction on blogs can occur between a small number of people. In a cynical view, the library blogosphere can tend toward being incestuous. This is true of ed-tech blogs as well, which intersect with library blogs. This is both a blessing and a curse in building a PLN. The benefit is the ability to serendipitously find new bloggers and fresh perspectives on common library and educational issues. On the other hand, it can be an intimidating environment. Furthermore, there can be a tendency to support one another's views, and to not engage in the realities facing many teacher-librarians. In other words, there is a tendency to "preach to the choir." However, when debate erupts in the blogosphere, it can be highly informative, opening new avenues of thinking and philosophy.

Developing Your Personal Blog Network

There are a number of ways to develop a robust collection of feeds and blogs that you read or from which you gather information on a daily basis. In fact, you may find that you need to edit your network as you get more comfortable using it, or find new feeds you wish to add. I have developed a "closet rule": one feed in, one feed out.

The first step to developing a network is to determine the type of information in which you are interested. For example, my aggregator is divided into folders for popular culture, news, books, and libraries and technology. You may want information on history or local news. You need to decide what you need to know and what will help you deliver the best services to your patrons. Because the Internet and the world of blogs have grown at such a quick rate, having an overall picture of your needs is an essential starting point. You should, however, remain open to additions you did not originally foresee.

A number of search engines may help if you do not know where to start. The most popular and familiar is Technorati. You can also search Google (under the more tab) or IceRocket. You may find that using a search engine to locate blogs of interest is tedious and time-consuming. However, setting up an RSS feed of tags you are interested in may help you manage a search. Tags are subject words decided on by the author and attached to entries. For more information, see the section on social bookmarking.

Another way is to use PLNs of bloggers to find people you might be interested in. In general you only need one blog of interest. Most bloggers also host a blogroll, which is a collection of links to blogs they read. By using the blogroll to connect to other interesting reads you will find yourself branching out into a social network that until the last five years was not particularly available to us.

As Figure 4.1 demonstrates, the blogosphere is an interconnected collection of data that is truly a web. By using the connections you can quickly build a personal network of daily reading, or weekly, that will give you food for thought, expand your repertoire, and provides tools you need to improve your service to patrons including the teaching strategies you employ.

Blogs As a Learning Experience

Getting the most out of your aggregator is a matter of identifying your needs, identifying the blogs that meet those needs, and becoming an active participant in the social experience. Beyond that perhaps the best we can do is to dedicate time for ourselves to contemplate. It is easy in a Web environment to "taste" what is available to us and move on without much consideration. Because of the ever-changing, updated nature of blogs it is even easier to consume information without integrating

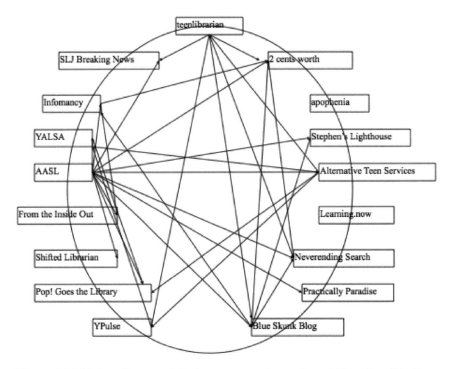

Figure 4.1 This is a diagram of the interconnectedness of one folder of my Bloglines subscriptions.

it into our knowledge. The time you have for contemplation should factor into your consideration of what feeds you have and how you manage them.

Using Google Reader or Bloglines will allow you to save posts to return to later or to use Bloglines to clip posts to save. Taking the time to contemplate what others are saying and to apply it to your situation is essential to professional growth.

Another way to enhance the experience is to become an active commenter on blogs that discuss professional issues. Commenting extends a conversation and allows you to hear other points of view. Often, comments will lead to further posts by the original writer exploring the comments. Although not every feed will be one you consider for commenting participation, in the professional realm comments should be a part of the reading if a post captures your attention. Although "lurking" is perfectly acceptable, comments are generally appreciated by writers, confirming that they are writing for an audience.

Another way to extend the experience of learning through blogs is to start one yourself. Writing will allow you to explore your thoughts on a given topic. You can share your thoughts with others in order to get feedback or you can keep your ideas private. Sharing your ideas will help you build a network and make connections with others who share your interests. However, even writing in private, an option available on most blogging software, will help you organize your thoughts and discover new ideas.

Blogs, and blogging, are excellent tools for expanding professional knowledge. One caveat in building a PLN of blogs is to consider adding blogs written by people who challenge the perception of the status quo. Although their point of view may be infuriating, challenging opinions will help flesh out your own. Teacher-librarians encourage students to investigate different points of view. By following the advice we impart we not only model information literacy, we improve our understanding of the value of multiple perspectives.

In the next section, blogs are annotated and recommended in a variety of fields including books and reading, information literacy, ed-tech, popular culture, and organizations.

Recommended Blogs

Books

Author Blogs

Authors are more accessible than ever and many maintain blogs. Author blogs range from self-promotion to their own daily ramblings and thoughts. They are often fun, humanizing the people behind the books, and are excellent to share with students who are their fans as well. This is a partial list of author's blogs, primarily those that are updated on a regular basis. The age ranges reflect the author's usual audience, not the readers of the blog.

Laurie Halse Anderson (http://halseanderson.livejournal.com/): Anderson is a prolific blogger. Her entries are primarily personal, but she encourages writing and provides the usual information regarding her books and appearances. (K–12)

Holly Black (http://blackholly.livejournal.com/): Black writes regularly with posts that range from personal to promotional information (such as book signings). (7–12)

Meg Cabot (http://www.megcabot.com/diary/): Cabot posts on a semi-regular basis. Her blog provides primarily promotional information, giveaways, and other items sprinkled with commentary on television, events in her life, and Henrietta (her very amusing cat). (5–12)

Sarah Dessen (http://writergrl.livejournal.com/): Dessen is a consistent blogger (although having a child has slowed her down a bit). She posts about the television programs she watches, daily events in her life, and the books she is reading. Hers is an excellent example of how an author becomes a "just like you and me" person. (9–12)

Finding Wonderland (http://writingya.blogspot.com/): "The writing YA weblog" is a collection of posts on issues in the YA world, publishing, and inspirations, as well as some other items the authors enjoy and want to share. (6–12)

Gail Giles (http://notjazz.livejournal.com/): Giles is a semi-regular poster. She posts about books she has read, personal experiences, and occasionally about her books and the many questions she fields regarding her choices, including where she gets her ideas. (8–12)

John Green (http://www.sparksflyup.com/weblog.php): Green is an occasional blogger. (Be sure and check out the Brotherhood 2.0 videos on YouTube and the nerdfighters Ning.) He posts videos, appearance information, process thoughts, and book information, as well as information on his personal interests. (9–12)

Interesting NonFiction for Kids (I.N.K.) (http://inkrethink.blogspot. com/): I.N.K. writers are nonfiction authors who write for children. Because there is not a large number of blogs in which nonfiction books are reviewed or discussed, entries into the field are welcome. The entries in this blog offer a philosophical approach so there is an element of learning about what it takes to write nonfiction and the writing process, as well as deeper reviews and examinations of some non fiction books. Many of the authors involved in posting in I.N.K. also host their own blogs worth exploring. (K–12)

Maureen Johnson (http://maureenjohnson.blogspot.com/): Johnson is a sporadic blogger, but her entries are usually longer. Although her topics are personal and include information about books and appearances, she also uses her blog for more creative writing (including a great piece about the YA mansion). (8–12)

Justine Larbalestier (http://justinelarbalestier.com/blog/): Larbalestier is a regular poster about all things that interest her. This blog is an excellent example of how reading an author's blog is a way to get to "know" the person behind the books, what interests the person has, what excites the person, or his or her pet peeves. Larbalestier also has a fabulous blogroll that will lead all over the Web to fun sites. (7–12)

e. lockhart (http://www.theboyfriendlist.com/e_lockhart_blog/): lockhart is a regular poster, and her blog is reflective of the blogosphere. She posts links to items of interest, completes memes, interviews other authors, and also posts information about her books and appearances. (8–12)

Barbara Johansen Newman (http://www.johansennewman.typepad. com/): Newman, a children's book author and illustrator, semi-regularly updates her blog with things she is interested in and adds pictures to illustrate her writing. (K–5)

Outside of a Dog (http://johansennewman.typepad.com/outside_of_ a_dog/): Several different writers share information about new books and new authors. (K–8)

Mitali Perkins (http://www.mitaliblog.com/): Similar to other author blogs, Perkins also addresses multicultural issues in children's literature. (K–8)

Cynthia Leitch Smith (http://cynthialeitichsmith.blogspot.com/): This is a frequently updated blog with giveaways, author interviews, tons of links, and information. It is an excellent starting place and a complete blog that will lead you to any number of places and people of interest in children's or young adult (YA) literature. (K–12)

Westerblog (http://scottwesterfeld.com/blog/): On Scott Westerfeld's blog, he posts news related to his books, musings on issues related to his books, and other general information his fans might be interested in. (7–12)

Mo Willems (http://mowillemsdoodles.blogspot.com/): This blog keeps you up to date on current projects by Willems, including his color commentary for the book cart drill team competition at the ALA conference. (K–6)

There are many more author blogs and by investigating blogrolls you may find your favorite author, so take some time to read author blogs, and find ones that you enjoy to add to your RSS feeder.

Reviews

The kidlit blogosphere, along with book networking communities such as Goodreads and LibraryThing have contributed to a sense of reading as a social activity. Readers are able to share reactions, read reviews, and participate in global conversations about children's and YA literature.

Abby the Librarian (http://abbylibrarian.blogspot.com/): This blog offers a range of reviews of both children's literature and YA nature and also includes information on programming.

American Indians in Children's Literature
(http://americanindiansinchildrensliterature.blogspot.com/):
Debbie Reese posts to this blog, which reviews children's books through the lens of Native American criticism. It is a "specialty" blog that investigates Native Americans in children's books; therefore it often has a different perspective on books than other reviewers.

As If (http://asifnews.blogspot.com/): Although not technically a review blog, this also is not strictly an author's blog. As If stands for Authors Supporting Intellectual Freedom and post entries and news regarding challenges to books and authors. It is updated as needed.

Becky's Christian Reviews (http://stand-firm-then.blogspot.com/): This blogger hosts a number of blogs, but I included this one because of its particular focus on Christian literature, which is not all that common in the kidlitosphere.

Big A, Little a (http://kidslitinformation.blogspot.com/): This is the blog of *The Edge of the Forest*, an online monthly journal that focuses on children's literature. It hosts reviews, links to other reviews, and is regularly updated.

Bildungsroman (http://slayground.livejournal.com/): Little Willow, the blog's author, is a prolific reader and blogger who posts reviews, links to events, and author interviews. The list of books she has read is impressive.

Bookshelves of Doom (http://bookshelvesofdoom.blogs.com/): This is a frequently updated blog of primarily YA literature and book news. It has links to current conversations, articles about book challenges, pop culture items, and book reviews.

A Chair, a Fireplace, and a Tea Cozy (http://yzocaet.blogspot.com/): This blog now has three contributors. The focus is on books for children and teens, but it hosts other posts generally related to popular culture. It is frequently updated, and weighs in thoughtfully on current debates in the literary world. It also has a very complete blogroll with numerous links to other sites and blogs.

Chasing Ray (http://chasingray.com/): Chasing Ray has lengthy, thoughtful reviews of current titles for both adult and young adults. The site also posts on the writing process, and current news in the literary world. The majority of her posts are long for a blog post, but her reviews are professional and provide in depth criticism.

Cybils (http://dadtalk.typepad.com/cybils/): The Cybils, a blogger's literary award for children's and young adult literature, began in 2006. The blog hosts reviews of the nominated titles, as well as other relevant posts. Categories include fantasy and science fiction, fiction picture books, graphic novels, middle grade fiction, nonfiction: middle grade and young adult, nonfiction picture books, and young adult books. It is a relatively quiet blog most of the year, except during the process.

A Fuse #8 Production (http://www.schoollibraryjournal.com/blogs. html): *SLJ* hosts a number of blogs including this one written by Elizabeth Bird. It is a kidlit blog, so it includes news, reviews, and items of interest to the kidlit world. The posts tend to be longer, and thoughtful rather than quick tidbits.

Guys Lit Wire (http://guyslitwire.blogspot.com/): This is a collaborative effort designed to bring attention to young adult literature that will interest teenaged boys. It has a large number of contributors; and although still new enough to be finding its footing, it updates regularly. It also includes links to unexpected sites that will appeal to teenage boys (and girls).

I'm a Reading Fool (http://readingfool.blogspot.com/): Included on this blog are occasional updates with lengthy reviews of young adult books.

Jen Robinson's Book Page (http://jkrbooks.typepad.com/): Robinson writes complete reviews of a wide variety of books on a regular basis. She crosses age levels and posts regularly as well as sending out a newsletter via e-mail.

Libriana: Great Books for Tweens and Teens (http://librarina. wordpress.com/): The benefit of this book review blog is that the books are not always the most recent, but it does have a nice range of older and newer titles.

MotherReader (http://www.motherreader.com/): MotherReader is home of the 48-Hour book Challenge, a collection of individuals who read and blog together during a 72-hour period. You choose the 48 hours during which you wish to participate. MotherReader is a prolific reader and blogger, who posts reviews of both children's and young adult literature as well as other book-related news (and an occasional personal post).

Nonfiction Matters (http://www.schoollibraryjournal.com/blogs. html): Another blog hosted on *SLJ*. Marc Aronson explores nonfiction and provides links to titles. He also discusses why librarians and youth advocates should be familiar with nonfiction and use it with their library users, and the comments extend this discussion in a thoughtful manner.

Read Roger (http://www.hbook.com/blog/): The blog of Roger Sutton, editor of *Horn Book*, contains book news rather than reviews, but often generates fascinating conversation in the comments.

Reading Rants! Out of the Ordinary Teen Booklists! (http://www. readingrants.org/): Originally a static Web site, Reading Rants migrated to the blogosphere to maximize the ability to interact while reviewing and discussing books. As a blog, the updates are more frequent than the Reading Rants static Web site, but not overwhelming in their number.

Seven Impossible Things Before Breakfast (http://blaine.org/ sevenimpossiblethings/): This blog features book reviews, spanning a wide variety and age designation of material, as well as plenty of author and illustrator interviews.

Wands and Worlds (http://www.wandsandworlds.com/blog1/): Wands and Worlds focuses on science fiction and fantasy for children and teens.

YA Fabulous (http://yafabulous.blogspot.com/): YA Fabulous indexes young adult reviews from an incredible number of blogs that feature reviews. This could be a good addition if you only need or want one young adult literature blog.

The YA YA YAs (http://theyayayas.wordpress.com/): This blog is written by three librarians on a regular basis with a focus on all things young adult including book news, books, and programming.

Education and Ed-Tech Blogs

The bloggers included in this section are a combination of practitioners and gurus, those who advocate for integration of newer technology tools. These blogs are primarily focused on the classroom, and some occasionally express a belief that libraries are outdated, which sparks conversation and debate.

Weblogg-ed (http://weblogg-ed.com/): Will Richardson's blog focuses on ed-tech issues. It is more theory than practical, but it can generate some ideas, and provide theoretical underpinning for integrating new technology tools.

2 Cents Worth (http://davidwarlick.com/2cents/): Similar to Richardson's blog, David Warlick examines current issues in public education, ed-tech, and educational policies.

Learning.Now (http://www.pbs.org/teachers/learning.now/): Hosted on PBS, this blog is written by Andy Carvin. It has lengthy posts that are in-depth explorations of ed-tech topics.

Spotlight: Blogging the Field of Digital Media and Literacy (http://spotlight.macfound.org/): Each week a different author highlights what is happening in the field of digital literacy.

Project New Media Literacies (http://newmedialiteracies.org/blog/): This blog highlights thoughts and explorations of "new media" and participatory culture.

Cool Cat Teacher (http://coolcatteacher.blogspot.com/): Written by an ed-tech enthusiast, this blog introduces new tools and new ways of looking at information using those tools. The enthusiasm can be contagious, and there is plenty of new information.

Always Learning (http://mscofino.edublogs.org/): This blog examines 21st Century literacies from the point of view of a teacher working with primary students and their teachers to integrate 21st Century skills.

The Strength of Weak Ties (http://strengthofweakties.org/): David Jakes authors this blog, which is a critical examination of technology and education. Jakes is recognized in the ed-tech community, but his posts are often critical analysis, offering a balance to pure enthusiasm.

Practical Theory (http://www.practicaltheory.org/serendipity/): Chris Lehmann, the principal at Science Leadership Academy, uses this blog to explore the current state of education and the theory underlying the assumptions and choices we make while educating our students.

Teacher Leaders Network Blogs (http://www.teacherleaders.org/featured-bloggers): This site features several bloggers from a wide range of disciplines and with a variety of interests.

Dangerously Irrelevant (http://www.dangerouslyirrelevant.org/): Scott McLeod is primarily interested in leadership issues and examples in education. The seemingly intended audience of this blog would be school administrators, but McLeod's examination of educational issues provides information for everyone to contemplate, as well as to lead readers to other links and educational news.

Students 2.0 (http://students2oh.org/): The "about us" statement identifies what makes this blog unique, and therefore a must-add to your reader. It is written by students. The entries thoughtfully examine the students' education experiences and education controversy from their own point of view. Unfortunately the volume of post had been drastically reduced as the students have moved on; they are recruiting new bloggers.

The Thinking Stick (http://www.thethinkingstick.com/): Although this could be labeled another ed-tech blog and it is, it also has the benefit of being written by someone with international school experience, thus it offers a more global examination of education.

Ideas and Thoughts from an EdTech (http://ideasandthoughts.org/): Sometimes a quick, few sentence post is what you need to get ideas flowing. This blog meets that need, although some posts are lengthy.

TechLearning (http://www.techlearning.com/blog/): This blog aggregates a number of authors who post in one place about ed-tech tools, implementation, and student skills.

Around the Corner (http://www.edsupport.cc/mguhlin/): Miguel Guhlin is an instructional technology director; his blog is both critical and enthusiastic about the role of instructional technologies, recognizing the tools needed to be thoughtfully embedded in curriculum.

Hundreds of educational and ed-tech blogs are available. In investigating any number of these blogs for consideration for adding to your RSS feeder you will find many more. While researching and evaluating the blogs in these lists, I found myself reading and learning, following links that led me far away from my original intention, opening up new avenues of inquiry, and being introduced to previously unread bloggers. Take some time to explore a few; to get lost in the blogosphere maze, it is worth the time it takes.

Library Blogs

It is difficult at times to separate ed-tech and library blogs as quite obviously there is some overlap. For the purpose of this book, I included in the library section those blogs written by people who have a particular interest in libraries, those who focus more on technology are located in the ed-tech section.

School Libraries

School Library Journal Blogs: These blogs can be found on the *SLJ* Web site (http://www.schoollibraryjournal.com/) and have a focus on school libraries.

Neverending Search, written by Joyce Valenza, focuses on information literacy, technology tools integrated into school libraries, and teaching opportunities, among others. It tends to have a secondary focus based on authorial experience, but there are things to be considered and learned at the elementary level.

Practically Paradise, written by Diane Chen, focuses more on elementary school libraries. This blog contains a number of reviews of children's books, as well as exploration of topics and issues of interest to all school libraries.

Independent School Library Blogs
Blue Skunk Blog (http://doug-johnson.squarespace.com/blue-skunk-blog/): This is a regularly updated blog that examines ed-tech and school library issues. Doug Johnson's posts often inspire thoughtful conversation, and he is an active participant in the digital conversation that occurs between bloggers.

Not So Distant Future (http://www.futura.edublogs.org/): This blog is updated on a regular basis with long posts that examine the pedagogy of new technologies in the library. The focus is on student learning and the processes and tools we can use to achieve results.

Infomancy (http://schoolof.info/infomancy/): Chris Harris comes from a background in instructional technology, and as such his blog tends to focus on the technology of school libraries. However, he is innovative, and this blog provides plenty of food for thought.

The Primary Source Librarian (http://www.maryjjohnson.com/primarysourcelibrarian/): This blog provides information on teaching with and integrating primary sources. It includes lesson plans, ideas, and news about new digitized resources.

The Unquiet Librarian (http://theunquietlibrarian.wordpress.com/): The focus of this blog is Web 2.0 tools with an emphasis on using the tools to improve library services and teaching in school libraries.

Teen Librarian Blog (http://teenlibrarianblog.blogspot.com/): Written by a middle school teacher-librarian, the posts cover a wide variety of topics that impact teaching and learning and school libraries.

Alice in Infoland (http://www.aliceinfo.org/): This blog is updated on a semi-regular basis with a variety of posts that explore new tools and other news that impacts school libraries and the students they serve.

A Library By Any Other Name (http://alibraryisalibrary.blogspot.com/): Conscientious poster of session notes and links from conferences attended, and the winner of the 2007 Edublog Award for Best Library Blog.

Digital Bookends (http://shonda.edublogs.org/): The lengthy posts on this blog examine the personal and professional issues that face many teacher-librarians.

California Dreamin' (http://robdarrow.wordpress.com/): Although Rob Darrow tends to blog more frequently about digital education and online learning as well as his own processes, he does have a library background. His blog is primarily ruminations about his professional experiences, learning, and information interests. His posts lead to interesting and new places.

Dunstanology (http://newdunstantoo.blogspot.com/): Updated on a semi-regular basis, these are personal reflections on school libraries. Conversations here are similar to what one might hear in the hallway at a conference, and the blog actively participates in conversation in the "hallway of the blogosphere."

Rhondda's Reflection Wandering About the Web (http://rhondda.wordpress.com/): This has two blog pages, one that focuses more on ed-tech in the library and the other that focuses on literature. It embeds video and gives concrete examples and new tools. It is a newer blog, but it is growing.

Wanderings (http://wanderings.edublogs.org/): Another teacher-librarian who is passionate about new technologies and school libraries writes this blog.

Organizational Blogs

AASLBlog (http://www.aasl.ala.org/aaslblog/): This blog is hosted by AASL and features organizational news and opportunities as well issues that impact teacher-librarians working in a variety of situations.

ACRLog (http://acrlog.org/): While the focus of this organization is higher education, the issues have resonance for K–12 educators as well.

ALSC (http://alsc.ala.org/blog/): Similar to AASL's blog, this ALSC blog focuses on organizational news, but also includes podcasts, musings about children's materials, and programming topics.

YALSA (http://yalsa.ala.org/blog/): Again this blog covers organizational news, but it also address issues of youth advocacy and serving teens in libraries, including information on programming, collection development, and technology. It also includes links to podcasts.

Library Blogs

These blogs are written with an emphasis on libraries and library services, but the focus is beyond school libraries and is primarily on public libraries.

The Shifted Librarian (http://theshiftedlibrarian.com/): The emphasis of this blog is Library 2.0, or how our role is changing in the new information age. It includes information and analysis of the new tools, new programming, and hot topics in "library land."

Stephen's Lighthouse (http://stephenslighthouse.sirsi.com/): Written by Stephen Abram of SIRSI Dynix, this blog is frequently updated with information on new studies and news that impact library services.

Pop! Goes the Library (http://www.popgoesthelibrary.com/): Authored by a number of people, the emphasis on the posts on this blog is how to keep current in popular culture and how to incorporate this into library services. Pop culture is an excellent way to connect with your students, and this blog helps make it easy.

Alternative Teen Services (http://www.yalibrarian.com/): Written by several teen service librarians, this blog discusses programming, books, and working with teens.

Librarilly Blonde (http://blogs.bccls.org/carlie/): Although the author of this blog writes in other places, she updates her personal blog regularly. The focus is on teens, and services as well as items of interest to teens. It also includes book reviews.

Librarian in Black (http://librarianinblack.typepad.com/librarianinblack/): This blog focuses on new technology tools that are of interest to librarians.

Library Storytime (http://librarystorytime.wordpress.com/): This blog focuses on programming for children's services. It is updated on a semi-regular basis.

News and Culture Blogs

News Feeds

Most news organizations offer news feeds including CNN, BBC, NPR, MSNBC, Reuters, and the Associated Press (AP). Having news feeds in your reader affords quick access to top headlines from news organizations, particularly Reuters and AP. Traditional newspapers also offer feeds, including *The New York Times*, the *Wall Street Journal, The Washington Post*, and the *Los Angeles Times*. Often, newspapers will offer feeds of a particular section. Furthermore, traditional news sources have embraced new media in offering blogs by columnists, which sometimes are available only online. News alerts, such as the one provided by Google, also can be set up. News alerts based on subjects selected by the user will be sent on a timetable the user requests.

Other online news sources include the following:

Salon (http://www.salon.com/): Salon offers breaking news as well as in depth articles that examine politics and culture.
Slate (http://www.slate.com/): Slate is similar to Salon but posts more, with a wider range of views. Salon is quite progressive in its political bias, Slate, less so; furthermore Slate is free.

Librarian's Index to the Internet (http://lii.org/): This blog provides a "What's New this Week" feed to the Web sites that the site indexes. The weekly updates often highlight sites that are related to current events, or are timely such as sites related to holidays or anniversaries of important events.

Popular Culture

You may wonder why there is a section on popular culture blogs in this volume? The mission of school libraries is primarily identified as supporting the standards and curriculum of the state and district, so what role does popular culture have in the school library? There are a number of different ways to answer that question. In today's climate there is a great deal of concern surrounding literacy; politically the U.S. government has focused improving the reading skills of our students, the media breathlessly reported the National Education Association Reading at Risk study which described a 10% decline in *literary reading*, and the teachers and other teacher-librarians we work with anecdotally tell stories about students who "hate to read." On the other hand Stephen Krashen, among others, remind us that access to books is necessary in order to encourage children's reading. I would argue that it isn't merely access, the books have to be of interest and the students need to know they are there. This, then, is how knowledge of popular culture is invaluable.

A teacher-librarian who is aware of which celebrities are popular, what movies their students are discussing, what television they insist on watching (and how), and what interests students express can provide supplemental print material to support those interests. This is particularly important in the tween years when research documents a decrease in the reading habits of students (particularly boys). Nonfiction titles on gaming, music, sports, or biographies are high-interest materials, which may encourage independent reading. Furthermore there are titles that receive "buzz"; often they are reviewed in magazines such as *Entertainment Weekly*. They are blogged about, and they have avid fans. They also will help bring students into the library. A student who passes through your doors to check out the latest book on skateboarding is likely to learn that the library has other materials that will meet his or her information needs. The teacher-librarian who knows who the latest Disney star is or what the score of the game was the night before builds credibility with students. You don't have to watch the game, you just have to know how it ended. And finally, teacher-librarians who tap into the culture of their students can use their knowledge to market the library, themselves, and the resources they provide. An awareness of popular culture can be a positive tool to have in a school library environment.

It is, however, difficult to keep up beyond a glance at the tabloid headlines while in line at the grocery store. Going farther than our personal television, music, movie, and sports interests can be daunting, and uninteresting to watch, read, and/or listen to. However a number of news sources, or popular culture blogs can make keeping up quite easy.

Sports

ESPN, CBS SportsLine, and Fox Sports all have news feeds that provide updated headlines in the world of sports. Each site also hosts blogs written by columnists and sports journalists. Identifying particular interests of students and using sports news feeds to keep current facilitates conversations, reader's advisory, and works as a collection development tool.

Movies, Music, and Television

YPulse (http://www.ypulse.com/): YPulse is directed at media and marketing professionals who are interested in tweens and teens, but there is plenty of valuable information about trends and interests of the middle and high school-age group. The host of YPulse is aware of the librarians in her audience and provides information valuable to that population as well. Links are provided to news articles and research reports as well as analysis. This is a go-to source.

PopWatch (http://popwatch.ew.com/popwatch/): The PopWatch blog is sponsored by *Entertainment Weekly* and hosts frequent updates about both "gossip items," current popular media, personal opinion of certain media, and news. Although it tends toward celebrity gossip, it has valuable information and is "safe for work."

Pop Matters (http://www.popmatters.com/): Pop Matters identifies itself as a "magazine of culture criticism." The reviews and articles are of less familiar items; but they range from mainstream media to comics and multimedia.

Pop Candy (http://blogs.usatoday.com/popcandy/): Hosted by *USA Today* and written by a columnist Whitney Matheson, Pop Candy keeps on top of what the "buzz" is in the world of popular culture.

Gawker Media

Gawker Media (GM) is an online media company founded and owned by Nick Denton and based in New York City. It is considered to be one of the most visible and successful blog-oriented media companies. As of

April 2008, it was the parent company for 12 different weblogs, including Gawker.com, Defamer, Fleshbot, Deadspin, Lifehacker, Gizmodo, Consumerist, io9, Kotaku, and Jezebel. The overarching tone of posts on most GM sites is sarcastic, and it has plenty of not safe for work (NSFW) postings. It tends toward gossip, not news as viewed by the mainstream media. Over the years, the sites have been criticized by the mainstream media for such things as violating privacy with reports of star sightings as they happen along with address, which are posted on Gawker or the gossipy, and occasionally nasty tone of the site (Buzz Bissinger on Deadspin during a Bob Costas interview). In defense of these sites, the criticism leveled at them are usually directed at those commentating, not the posters; but it can cross between the two worlds. Still, the overwhelming popularity and the role GM has come to play in our cultural lexicon is worth being aware of. Although I hesitate to recommend adding GM sites to blogrolls, I find that I use them as a way to stay current with popular culture, and as a way to truly be able to participate in the new media versus traditional media debate. I would be remiss in not bringing the reader's attention to these sites.

Blogs for Fun

Some days we need a break. These blogs are included as "just for fun" blogs; feeds to add to your aggregator.

Cute Overload (http://cuteoverload.com/): This very popular site consists primarily of photographs and video of baby animals, but also includes grown animals doing adorable things.

National Geographic (http://news.nationalgeographic.com/index.rss): You can receive *National Geographic* news updates using this RSS feed.

Digital Journalist (http://digitaljournalist.org/blog/category/galleries/): Digital Journalist is a site for photojournalism; the blog hosts images from the webzine. If you are interested in photography this hosts interesting photos.

Flickr Blog (http://blog.flickr.net/en): Flickr is a social network that shares photography. The blog posts interesting images as well as news about Flickr. For the images alone, the blog is worth a peek.

I can has cheezburger (http://icanhascheezburger.com/): Using photographs of cats with funny captions, this popular site can be not safe for work (NSFW), particularly if you are working with elementary students, but it contains some funny pictures and captions.

Post Secret (http://postsecret.blogspot.com/): Post Secret is not a secret anymore. Several successful books compile the art work. This blog posts some of the secrets online. The concept behind Post Secret was an art display in which people submitted secrets on postcards. The secrets are funny, sad, poignant, bitter, and sometimes horrifying; the range of human emotions and experiences. This blog is definitely NSFW for K–12 educators.

Manolo's Shoe Blog (http://shoeblogs.com/): Admittedly, this is a personal choice, but I included it to demonstrate that the Web has a number of fashion blogs that are smart and funny. This blog is obviously about shoes, although the Manolo hosts a number of other fashion blogs, and links to others.

Unshelved (http://www.unshelved.com/): Did you know you can get a RSS feed of the popular library comic Unshelved? Follow Dewey and his co-workers at Mallville library in a daily update.

Dr. Horrible's Sing Along Blog (http://www.drhorrible.com/): This is Joss Whedon's answer to the Hollywood writer's strike starring Neil Patrick Harris as Dr. Horrible (who may actually be a good guy), Nathan Fillion, and Felicia Day.

TWITTER[1]

Twitter, or short-message service (SMS) blogging, is a cross between text messaging and blogging. Using Twitter is also referred to as microblogging because updates, or "tweets" must be 140 characters or less.

Twitter is a relative newcomer to the scene, founded in 2006, but quickly embraced by early adopters. It can be updated from the Web or your phone. A number of Twitter applications, or open source applications designed to work with Twitter make using it more functional.

Building a Twitter Network

Without building a focused network of people you follow, Twitter may be interesting; but it is useless. By selecting people to follow you can set

[1] There are other SMS services such as Pownce.

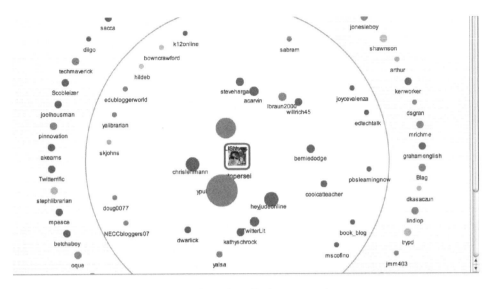

Figure 4.2 This is a visual representation of my Twitter network.

up Twitter (or a Twitter desktop application) to send you tweets only from your friends. The public timeline tweets from around the world at a pace impossible to keep up with. Furthermore, adding friends enables you to get tweets from people in whom you are interested, in a language you can read because you can Twitter in all languages. Finding friends can be done with a keyword search, but it is helpful to have a starting place (i.e., my Twitter name is: Mtnpersei). Figure 4.2 is a representation of my personal Twitter network as of July 2008, the larger the dot the more frequent the tweets.

You can view the profile of the people you are following, which allows you to see who they are following and add from their list. This is true of people who begin to follow you as well. When building your Twitter network, look for people who use Twitter *primarily* for professional purposes as those posts will be most helpful.

You can also use applications built to search Twitter for people

- TwitDir (http://twitdir.com/) is a searchable directory.
- Twello is a "phone book" (http://www.twellow.com/).

Twitter As a Useful Service

Installing a Twitter desktop application allows Twitter to be truly useful and to be less time-consuming. Several of these applications are available, but the most popular is Twhirl, which runs on your desktop, and gives you audio and visual notification of new tweets. Other similar applications include Twitterific for Macs (which must be purchased) and Twitbin, which can run as a sidebar in your browser. Tweetdeck (http://www.tweetdeck.com) is another application that can be installed on a desktop. Tweetdeck allows the user to organize tweets into groups so that it is easier to follow conversations. The group capability is particularly useful. You can also install a Twitter widget on an iGoogle homepage. (iGoogle will be discussed in the final chapter.) Using one of these tools allows Twitter to run continuously and to be pushed out to you. You can find applications on the Twitter Fan wiki (http://twitter.pbwiki.com/).

Once you have arranged to receive tweets from friends, or other professionals, you may ask what now? In terms of advancing your professional knowledge, Twitter can act similar to an RSS aggregator. Often, users will post when they have posted a new blog entry. Users will link to other posts, or news stories that are relevant to their professional community, which is why it is helpful to add people focused on ed-tech, as well as on libraries. Twitter is probably the fastest way to stay updated on breaking news, which may or may not have relevance in your professional world. Tweets will lead you to new sites, new information, and help you stay current. You can also loosely follow tweets from a conference being attended by Twitterers.

Twitter Use As a Sandbox

Like most of the applications discussed in the Web 2.0 section of this book, using Twitter and Twitter applications is professional development in and of itself. While building a PLN, Twitter helps keep you current and connected, relieving isolation. Helping with the process of building one is a learning experience in and of itself. As you use Twitter (or wikis, blogs, aggregators, social bookmarking, etc.) you are learning. As you learn how to use an application and connect with other users, you learn how to integrate the service into your program, garner new ideas on teaching with different tools, or how to provide patron services using that tool. Even if you discover the tool does not work for you, and some will not, you will have an understanding of how it is used. Twitter is an application that you can use as a "sandbox" in which to learn. It is easy to learn and simple to trial. Establishing a group to follow, based on the recommendations, and installing a desktop tool, will quickly help you establish whether or not Twitter is a tool that will work for you. Furthermore, the 140-character limit on messages requires little in terms of posting. It can be a nonthreatening entry into sharing your thoughts, requiring very little writing, and limited feedback unless or until you build a solid network of followers.

In later chapters, I discuss managing information flow using a personal home page, most of which have Twitter "widgets," a piece of software integrated onto the page that pulls in tweets to that page. Installing a widget on an information management tool such as a home page renders the ability to "play in the sandbox" with Twitter even easier. A number of ways are available to experience Twitter (or Pownce); and it can be a less time-consuming exposure to the social nature of PLNs.

Twitter Recommendations

As identified previously, there are a number of ways to identify Twitters whose posts you may be interested in. Many of the bloggers I recommended also use Twitter and post information on their blog site regarding their Twitter account. The recommendations here are primarily Twitterers who post links to blogs or professional items. Many post tweets that are of a mixed nature—personal and professional.

General Interest

- CNN offers multiple Twitter feeds, including breaking news.
- Nprnews provides news updates from National Public Radio.
- Andy Carvin writes prolific tweets, updates current and breaking news, and links to articles and information.
- NewsHour posts tweets from the *NewsHour with Jim Lehrer*.
- *The New York Times* offers multiple Twitter feeds from sections of the traditional newspaper.
- ESPN updates sports headlines.

Libraries and Ed-Tech

- LISNews has consistent tweets with links to articles and blog posts of interest to librarians.

- Willrich45 contains Will Richardson's tweets of his experiences with technology, new tools and applications he has learned, and links to articles and blogs related to his interests.
- Lbraun2000 offers a large number of tweets, primarily professional and many links to articles and blog posts.
- Edtechtalk posts reminders of webcasts beginning on edtechtalk.
- Pbslearningnow is a Twitter feed that informs followers about updates of Andy Carvin's posts on the Learning.now blog hosted on the PBS Web site.
- Infogdss29 provides information and tweets regarding teen services, with emphasis on gaming.
- AngelaMaiers is an education consultant with a focus on literacy and tweets usually reflect an enthusiasm for the tools she discovers, as well as educational practices.
- YALSA is the Twitter feed of YALSA blog posts.
- Ypulsestasia hosts YPulse and extends her blog posts with tweets, which lead to resources, as well as YPulse news.
- Yalibrarian is the Twitter feed of blog posts as well as tweets of other links to professional items of interest.

Although there is a social component for blogs, wikis, and SMS blogging, they are different tools than the social tools designed for networking. Wikis are collaborative, blogs allow for commenting, and there are conversations that occur in SMS blogging. Each of these tools can however operate in isolation; no one may visit your blog or your wiki, although we would hope that is not the case. In the next chapter we will explore the tools that are designed more for building communities, for communicating, and sharing interests.

CHAPTER 5
Social Bookmarking and Social Networking

This chapter presents social bookmarking and social networking. A key component of Web 2.0 is the ease with which one can collaborate and communicate with others in a global society. The social nature of the tools has allowed building a PLN to become easier, and the members of the network have become (potentially) more diverse. The tools discussed in this chapter are about making connections and sharing information.

A DEFINITION OF SOCIAL BOOKMARKING

Social bookmarking is one of the first Web 2.0 applications to gain popularity and cause consternation in the traditional library world. Social bookmarking applications allow the user to save bookmarks on a Web server, making them available from *any* computer. It is the first example of cloud computing, in which Web servers host applications and/or documents making them accessible from any desktop. In social bookmarking applications users organize their bookmarks by tagging each entry. Tags, or keywords, are searchable and can be organized into a list or a tag cloud. Tags are not necessarily a single word, and can often be a phrase. Bookmarks that have been saved and tagged can be shared with a particular user of the same service or with other users who search tags and find the bookmarked links with the same tag.

Tagging is similar to cataloging, but instead of using a standard subject heading or taxonomy, users create their own subjects. This language has been dubbed "folksonomy" and has some serious disadvantages, as well as some positive aspects. The obvious advantage for any user is the access to bookmarks no matter what computer they are working on, but there are other advantages as well that will help build a professional library network.

PROS AND CONS OF FOLKSONOMIES AND BOOKMARKING

Librarians have struggled with the role the World Wide Web plays in the information landscape. In some cases, the Internet has been enthusiastically embraced, warts and all. In others, it is regarded with wariness, and occasionally disdain. In 1994, while most embraced online public access catalogs (OPACs), Nicholson Baker famously bemoaned the loss of the card catalog. In the early years of the verb "googling," we complained about the overreliance on Google. Web 2.0 applications have undergone the same debate. Perhaps the most popular is the role of Wikipedia. Before Wikipedia, however, there was a debate, hand-wringing or enthusiastic embrace, of folksonomies. Tagging was popularized by the social bookmarking site Delicious and the photo-sharing site Flickr. It was most often referenced in conversations of Flickr, but it has caught on across the social web.

On the positive side, tagging items with subjects that a user will remember or that means something to the user allows for an easier organization of pictures, Web sites, and others. The user will always be able to return to a necessary item by using his or her personally generated tags. Furthermore, there is a common language aspect to folksonomies. Users will gravitate toward common keywords. Some social bookmarking sites make this easier by identifying recommended tags or popular tags based on what other users have used for tagging the same site. It is not necessary to be a cataloger or have a master's degree in information science to use tagging, and therein lies the problem.

As demonstrated in Figure 5.1, folksonomies have no standardization. Although some grassroots organization and common keywords have emerged, there is still a cluttered, unpredictable aspect to relying on the masses to categorize items. Although using tags for organizing personal items is a handy tool, unpredictability is problematic when sharing or searching based on tags. Although one user might categorize a site as Web2.0, other variations will include Web2, Web 2.0, social web, readwriteweb, or even read_write_web. Sometimes the service will limit how tags are written, requiring them to be one word. Improved searching tools help eliminate some of the difficulties by suggesting tags that are similar in the searching but searching tags still lacks the convenience of searching a formalized taxonomy.

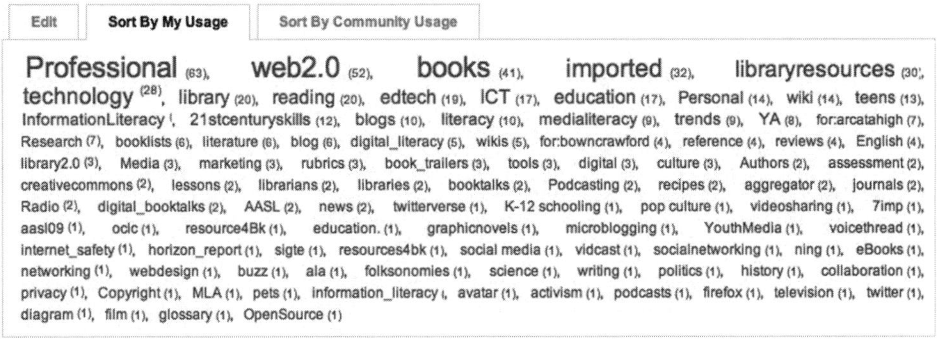

Figure 5.1 An example of a tag cloud.

The viability of a keyword as usable is dependent on the community that springs up around that keyword. If no one uses that particular tag, its usefulness for social networking is nonexistent, and it is nothing more than an organizational tool. On the other hand, if a tag is popular it *may* be rendered useless by the overwhelming results that are attached to it. In the ideal social Web world, a tag will help build a community that shares information that is relevant and valuable.

SOCIAL BOOKMARKING APPLICATIONS

Social bookmarking has a large number of applications. The application you choose will depend on the features you want to work with, the ease of the interface, and perhaps what other members of your PLN use. You will be able to choose between Delicious, Furl, Simpy, Diigo, and Clipmarks.

Social Bookmarking Applications

Delicious
  http://delicious.com/
Furl
  http://www.furl.net/
Simpy
  http://www.simpy.com/
Diigo
  http://www.diigo.com
Clipmarks
  http://clipmarks.com/

Delicious and Furl are similar applications that allow you to book-mark, tag, annotate, and share Web sites. Furl was unveiled in 2003, Delicious in 2004. Furl's annotation feature is more clearly defined, but Delicious allows you to add notes. Although Furl allows you to share with friends and has groups created around topics, Delicious al-lows you to build a network and send links to other people in your network. Delicious is more common in the K–12 and library commu-nities, and therefore has a larger user base with which to build your PLN. This is an excellent tool for sharing information with members of your PLN who use Delicious. Simpy is a similar service, but also employs clearly defined groups and a search mechanism for people who maintain Simpy accounts.

Diigo, another social bookmarking site, goes beyond sharing and organizing bookmarks. It allows you to highlight, make notes using digital sticky notes and annotate Web pages, making it an excellent tool for conducting research. By highlighting and placing digital sticky notes a user can return to a Web site and quickly find the reason for bookmarking the page. It also has tools to help you build a community of people who share your interests, making it a cross between a social networking site like MySpace or Facebook and a bookmarking site such as Furl or Delicious. Other social bookmarking sites that may suit your needs are available, and many of the existing sites continually upgrade services so that services in Diigo are becoming available in Delicious, and vice versa. Again, you should determine which tool you are com-fortable with and use it to maximize your interactions with people who can provide support, new ideas, and opposing views to consider.

Digg

Digg (digg.com) is not necessarily a social bookmarking site because it does not collect your personal bookmarks. It does, however, encourage conversation surrounding popular Web sites, and is an excellent way to stay current on the "buzz" of the Internet. Digg allows users to post stories and then vote on them, "Digg" for those they like, bury those they don't. Users can also comment on stories. The most popular stories, those with the most "Diggs" make the home page, which can be received as a feed. The concern with Digg is that it is a user-driven site; and stories that make the home page are not always accurate, relevant, or appropriate. Still a Digg feed or occasional visit will quickly identify popular stories, buzz in the digital community, and even what is dominating the American cultural consciousness.

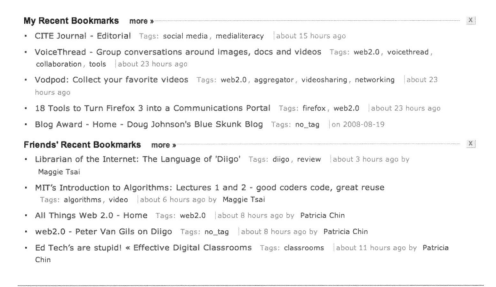

Figure 5.2 Diigo bookmarks from author and friends.

USING SOCIAL BOOKMARKING TO EXPAND
YOUR PERSONAL LEARNING NETWORK

Even if you are a teacher-librarian who is comfortable and familiar with Web 2.0 tools, you may not be comfortable using the tools to expand your network. Social bookmarking has excellent potential as a tool for our students and teachers. It's also an excellent tool for keeping current in our field. Using it as a professional development tool has distinct advantages in connecting us with other teacher-librarians, expanding our knowledge base, and as an organizational tool. By setting up RSS feeds for tags or keywords that we are interested in following, we can expand both our access to diverse resources and our PLN. Diigo, Delicious, and similar tools expand our network by offering the opportunity to search for users who share our interests and add them as "friends." Figure 5.2 is a screenshot of the author's bookmarks, as well as the recent bookmarks of my "friends." By sharing bookmarks, my knowledge of Web sites that interest me expands. It is not necessary to visit each site as tags and annotations allow a user to scan for relevant sites.

Another way to benefit from social bookmarks in a professional development sense is to set up a feed in your aggregator for certain keywords. This is a similar process to setting up feeds for blogs as tag

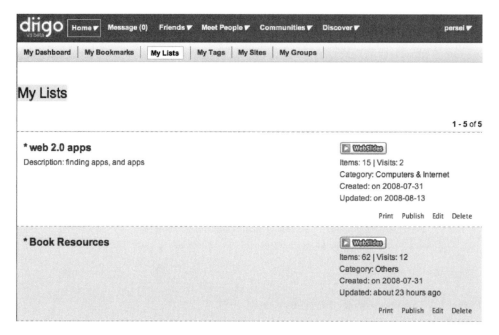

Figure 5.3 Diigo is an excellent research tool as highlights appear whenever you access a page.

searches are available in RSS. This will give you an idea of what other members of the community, interested in the chosen tag, are saving. It may lead you to a new research study, article, video, or Web site. Each new piece of information is a chance to expand your knowledge base and therefore improve your teaching or library program.

Annotating Web Sites

Diigo, and other services allow you to annotate, clip, or highlight Web pages. This is an excellent way to save and record your thoughts while reading a Web site. Diigo allows you to install a tool bar on your browser. Using this toolbar a user can highlight a Web page, automatically sending that page to a user's collection of bookmarks. In Figure 5.3 I have highlighted the words My Lists; when I visit that page on my local machine those words remain highlighted. As you are viewing a site you can bookmark it, and open up a sidebar that allows you to see others who have bookmarked that site as well as what comments they have made. Furthermore, Diigo allows you to post "sticky notes" that will be there when you return to the site, and that can be made public or kept private.

Google also provides a way to annotate Web sites using their Notebook. Installing Google Notebook on your browser allows you to clip a Web site and add a note. It saves the links to the sites you have marked and annotated. The flaw is that it tends to be computer-dependent.

Zotero is another service that uses a browser extension; unfortunately only for the browser Mozilla Firefox. The advantage of Zotero is that it is designed for academics, providing the citation as well as the ability to annotate, attach items, tag, and list related items. Zotero is a more complete service than Google Notebook, but is also computer-dependent. This service has plans for account management that will allow users to log in to Web sites and see their saved items, as well as share with other users.

Social Bookmarking As a Patron Service

Social bookmarking is an excellent tool for finding the unexpected site. Although this book is not meant to suggest tools for patron services, it is worth mentioning that you can develop a social bookmarking site for your teachers and students. You can encourage them to bookmark to the library's bookmarks, annotate bookmarks you provide, and therefore expand the resources you offer. It might also lead to previously unknown people in your community with whom you share similar interests or resources. By providing this patron service you may find local community members who can become part of your PLN.

As a tool for saving and sharing information, uncovering relevant resources (both popular and obscure), organizing information, and providing patron services, social bookmarking is an essential tool in the library of the new millennium. Social networks discussed next have received the most media attention, although most of it negative, but also have potential for libraries, and certainly for expanding your learning network in a global community.

SOCIAL NETWORKS

In truth, a PLN is merely a social network that you have built around professional connections. Many of the tools mentioned in social bookmarking are also social networking tools, however for the purpose of this chapter, social networks will reference tools that are designed for communication that include personalized home pages, groups, and the ability to blog, among others, and that are considered as primarily social networking sites. The applications I examine in this chapter are modeled on the success of MySpace and Facebook.

Both MySpace and Facebook have received a lot of press, particularly in terms of children, teens, and personal safety. They have potential for PLNs but are general applications that have a limitation of being too big to be truly useful in a professional development sense. However, they can be used, and I address that later in this chapter.

Nings

Ning is an online platform where a user can create a focused social network. For example, Joyce Valenza has created Teacher-Librarian Ning, which has more than 1,800 members and is growing. As a social community, a Ning also includes other groups of interest and the ability to connect with and "friend" other users. Forums spring up around common topics and users can post content, including videos and blogs. A Ning for teacher-librarians (and there is more than one) is a PLN in and of itself.

There are a number of ways to maximize a Ning. For one, a feed can be set up to notify you when a group that interests you has updated by adding new members or a new post. This helps Nings become "push technology" that comes to you rather than to another site that you have to visit on a regular basis to remain updated. You can search for and select or start a new group that has a particular focus that is of interest to you.

Elementary school teacher-librarians may not find a high school group helpful. However, peeking in on conversations in areas outside one's main interest is never a bad idea; you just might want to limit your time in the interest of information management. Do not be afraid to connect with strangers, to "friend" someone who looks interesting or shares a similar situation. You can learn from one another. When "friending" someone, make sure they are active members; you will get more from the active members rather than the occasional visitor. Keep an eye on the forums (yes, they have RSS) where questions are asked and discussions occur. Of course, one of the best things you can do is spend some time playing; learn the application and how it works. Keep in mind the question, "How can this be useful?"

Suggested Nings to Investigate

Teacher-Librarian Ning (http://teacherlibrarian.ning.com/): Members—1,832*

Library Youth and Teen Services 2.0 (http://libraryyouth.ning.com/): Members—288*

Library 2.0 (http://library20.ning.com/): Members—3,255*

Classroom 2.0 (http://www.classroom20.com/): Members—10, 575*

Nerdfighters (http://nerdfighters.ning.com/): Members—11,571*

* As of August 2008, most of these Nings are growing every day.

WebJunction

WebJunction, an online community for libraries, was mentioned in the section on online learning because of the webinars it provides. Like so many of these sites, WebJunction serves multiple purposes, including building a library community on the Web. WebJunction also hosts discussion boards (forums), a WebJunction wiki, and a member directory. Initially funded by a grant, it is sponsored by OCLC and is still partially grant funded. It is primarily for public libraries and holds nominal relevance to school libraries. However, school libraries in its partner states may find it more useful, than those who live in states who have not partnered with WebJunction. Furthermore, many universities are partnering with WebJunction to provide CE and professional development. Collaboration with public and school libraries can be overlooked. A visit to WebJunction may help build relationships with public libraries.

LinkedIn, Facebook, and MySpace

Facebook and MySpace are social entities, but there are business applications as well. Many authors and book groups have MySpace and Facebook pages. "Friending" authors or a book club such as Readergirlz may help you stay on top of current literature. You can add applications to your pages such as Visual Bookshelf that allow you to share what you are reading and receive recommendations. Libraries also maintain MySpace and Facebook pages that you can "friend." In truth, the size and focus do not make Facebook or MySpace good tools for professional development, although they have a role in patron services so are worth learning about. One more caveat, most schools filter access to social networking sites, and if not all sites, in particular MySpace and Facebook. LinkedIn is the businessman's Facebook. The profile you build on LinkedIn is based on your professional history. LinkedIn connects you with people in your profession. Because its focus is professional, it has a cleaner interface with less ability to "pretty up your page," but provides better connections within the profession.

As discussed in the next section on book networks, there are social networks that have a more directed focus and members who share similar characteristics. One example would be Eduspaces (http://eduspaces.net/), a social networking site dedicated to teachers and the education community. It may be a site to investigate, rather than the more general LinkedIn, Facebook, or MySpace communities. Social networking sites have the potential to connect teacher-librarians throughout the world, as well as connecting with other teachers, members of the community, students, and other stakeholders. Social networks also have the potential to connect readers, as I examine in the next section.

BOOK NETWORKS

How many times have you wondered what others think about the book you just finished reading, or wished you could get a recommendation based on what you have read from another reader with similar taste? Have you wondered if you are the only reader who doesn't understand why a book is popular? Book networks can provide these services for you. Based on the success of large, generalized social networks, a number of focused social networks have sprung up in the Web 2.0 landscape. Different from Nings because they are not user-created but are actual Web applications, they show promise for connecting teacher-librarians and expanding our access to professional information.

In particular, book networks can be extremely helpful to teacher-librarians. The concept allows you to share your books and reviews online. As one of our roles is to promote reading, book networks provide an excellent chance for teacher-librarians to connect with other readers for recommendations and reviews.

Applications

In 2005, LibraryThing was launched. Developed as a personal online library catalog, this application allows you to add books to a personal

Figure 5.4 LibraryThing profile for Mtnpersei.

catalog, tag the books with keywords (folksonomy), rate the books, and post comments and reviews. You can share your book reviews, see what other users have rated them, and review common titles.

LibraryThing provides the opportunity to swap books, receive recommendations, and discuss books from other users. Figure 5.4 is a screenshot of a library maintained on LibraryThing. Users create a profile similar to the profile in Figure 5.5. Although you can share your library, join groups, and participate in shared conversation about a book, LibraryThing is more of an online catalog than a social network because you don't add friends.

If you are currently a LibraryThing user for personal purposes and wish to maximize the application for professional development purposes, scan the groups that host focused forums, including Librarians who LibraryThing, Read YA Lit, and Children's Literature.

Shelfari, founded one year after LibraryThing, is a similar Web application. One difference is the ability to add friends. Shelfari is currently smaller than LibraryThing, which has the advantage of being less overwhelming, but it is not as easy to make connections because of LibraryThing's popularity. As usual, when making a decision the user interface may play a role, which design is easier for you to use.

Goodreads is another book network, smaller than LibraryThing but bigger than Shelfari. The difference in Goodreads is that you can manage three shelves by default—Read, Currently Reading, and To Be Read. You can also add shelves. You can connect with friends, join

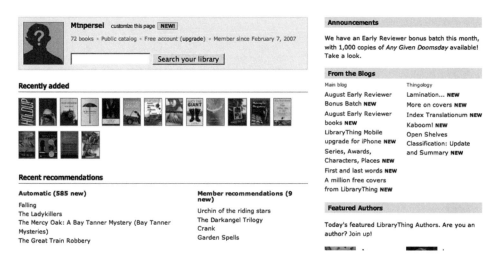

Figure 5.5 LibraryThing can display the covers, and your written reviews of the books you have added to your library.

groups, and browse book titles by a variety of different means. Figure 5.6 is a screen shot of the author's library as an example of the differences between Goodreads and LibraryThing's user interface.

On Goodreads, a user relies on friends for recommendations because this is not a recommendation engine like on LibraryThing. Also unlike LibraryThing and Shelfari, Goodreads is not a cataloging tool. Although it has book information, the other two include Dewey classification and Library of Congress information on a book. In order to help you understand Goodreads, I have posted my profile in Figure 5.7.

TAKING ADVANTAGE OF BOOK NETWORKS

Readers advisory is an important part of a teacher-librarian's job. On a number of occasions, the school library may be the only place in the school that promotes the concept of reading *for pleasure*. This is particularly true in a secondary school. One of the isolating factors of being a teacher-librarian on a school site is working with teachers who do not share our passion for reading what our students read. Even if we work with teachers who embrace children's and young adult literature, they often look to us for recommendations on the latest and the greatest. A number of ways are suggested in this book to connect with others to discuss books—listservs, broad networking

			rating	read	reviewed
God Went to Beauty School (Paperback)	Rylant, Cynthia	★★★★☆	read [edit]	3.97	Jul 25 ⊠ edit
Where the Heart Is (Paperback)	Letts, Billie	★★★★☆	read [edit]	3.72	Jul 25 ⊠ edit
Double Helix (Puffin Sleuth Novels)	Werlin, Nancy*	★★★★☆	read [edit]	3.59	Jul 25 ⊠ edit
Black Mirror (Paperback)	Werlin, Nancy*	★★★☆☆	read [edit]	3.60	Jul 25 ⊠ edit
Locked Inside (Paperback)	Werlin, Nancy*	★★★★☆	read [edit]	3.90	Jul 25 ⊠ edit
The Year My Sister Got Lucky (Hardcover)	Friedman, Aimee	★★★☆☆	read [edit]	3.89	Jul 25 ⊠ edit

Figure 5.6 Goodreads interface.

Figure 5.7 My profile on Goodreads.

sites, blogs, and others—but a membership on a book network can be the easiest way to keep yourself connected. You can share opinions, pet peeves, and recommendations with others who have similar situations. You can tap into their expertise as readers or as teacher-librarians. Two aspects of using your PLN for professional development is to connect and make it relevant. Book networks fill that need, reducing the sometimes isolating experiences we have.

You can use a book network to help with collection development. Relying solely on a book network will probably not fit with your selection policy, but you can use it to gain a better understanding, beyond a professional review about a book. Investigate what others have said about the titles. Look for recommendations and then use links to access professional reviews. Connect with other librarians to see what is popular in their area, and investigate adding those books to your collection.

You can also use a book network to supplement your reader's advisory. Although we cannot necessarily read everything in our library or even what is new, we can use PLN to gather other's opinion on books. You can use their recommendations to recommend books to our patrons, *just make it clear to them that you haven't read the book in order to maintain authenticity*. You can pose questions and share recommendation for a difficult patron. Even if you are not a reader, a book network is an excellent tool for staying on top of books, and helping with reader's advisory and collection development.

SECOND LIFE

Second Life is a virtual environment, a three-dimensional world of virtual beings that participate in the environment in much the same ways we interact in face-to-face real environments. Second Life allows one to build an avatar, and an identity that allows you to participate in the user-built environment. Many universities and libraries have begun to experiment with Second Life or Teen Second Life (the island built for teens, which employs more restrictions and works to reduce access to "adult content" as well as allow teens to build an environment for teens). For teacher-librarians, Second Life offers a way to connect in a virtual environment, to attend classes or lectures, to enter discussions, and to participate in the conversations with others interested in this virtual world and its implications for education.

The current concern is that more than one person has described Second Life's learning curve as more of a "learning cliff." For users not familiar with role-playing games, in particular Massively Multiplayer Online Role-Playing Game (MMORPG), Second Life can take quite a bit of time to learn to navigate. This can be particularly true of Mac users as the design of the environment is based on Windows commands.

In summer 2008, Google launched Lively, its version of Second Life. By the end of 2008 Google announced that they would no longer provide the Lively service. In an article reviewing Lively and comparing it to Linden Lab's Second Life, *Slate* magazine referenced "churn." Churn rate is described as people who log in to try the service but seldom, if ever, return (http://www.slate.com/id/2196199/). The amount of churn in Second Life and other virtual worlds makes it difficult to determine the "payoff" of learning Second Life to be able to participate in the virtual learning and conversation that occurs. However, the enthusiastic embrace by some universities, as well as libraries and library organizations, makes Second Life worth investigating.

- *For more information regarding Second Life and libraries visit http://infoisland.org/*
- *For more information about K–12 education in Second Life visit ISTE's Web site > Membership> Member Networking or SimTeach http://www.simteach.com/*

The ability to network with others, to share new ideas is one of the most powerful aspects of the Internet, and as it comes of age more tools and new ways of making those connections are becoming available. The virtual worlds of Second Life, the directed network of a Ning, or the ability to share book recommendations are all harbingers on the networks we will be seeing in the future. But, with the exception of Second Life, and recognizing that you can add video and audio to most profiles within social networking sites, the tools we have explored thus far are primarily text-based. In the next chapter we explore podcasts, vodcasts, and streaming video.

CHAPTER 6
Multimedia: On the Web

This chapter focuses on audio and video opportunities for learning in Web 2.0. Podcasts, and streaming online radio shows, are an integral part of a PLN, and videos and video streaming are becoming increasingly popular. With increased bandwidth, and faster connections, the Web has moved beyond a text-based interface, and is embracing the ability to easily post audio and video.

In the section on online courses, I discussed iTunes U as a possible source for professional development. The 1.0 nature of iTunes U is watching video without interaction in a one-time event. Other sites provide presentations with the opportunity for interaction or videos to which the user may respond. As you immerse yourself in a PLN you may find that these arenas work best if you prefer auditory learning. Podcasts, videos, online chats, and some mashup of all three can be an important part of the learning piece of your PLN.

PODCASTS

A podcast is a digital recording available for online distribution and available for download. The growth and popularity of podcasting began in 2004, and quickly became a fundamental piece of people's digital lives. Podcasts can be like listening to a radio show, either with one person sharing their ideas and perspectives in an auditory format, or it can include interviews or panels. Podcasts can be found by using Apple iTunes, which is available for PCs as well, or by searching the Podcast

Directory (http://www.podcastdirectory.com/). Similar to other Web 2.0 products, you can subscribe to a podcast that you enjoy. In some instances podcasts are hosted as weekly "Internet Radio Shows" which allow participation in real-time using chat. Podcasts are archived and you can read the chats as you listen. The benefit of a podcast is its portability, and for an auditory learner there is much to be gained.

VIDCASTS/VODCASTS

A vidcast is similar to a podcast, only it is video. Online videos have become a mainstream event, particularly with the popularity of YouTube, another popular social service often filtered out on K–12 school campuses. The ed-tech community recognized the value of digital video early on, and developed a number of vidcast channels, available through different services. UStream is one such resource, although it is not exclusively ed-tech related.

USTREAM TV Channels

- Will Richardson: http://www.ustream.tv/willrich45
- EdTechPosse: http://www.ustream.tv/channel/edtech-posse-live
- EdTechLive: http://www.ustream.tv/channel/edtechlive

A similar resource is WizIQ, which has public sessions. Another free resource for education-related videos is TeacherTube. Although it does not host "TV shows" in the fashion of UStream, users can rate and comment on videos in the manner of YouTube. A bonus is that TeacherTube is not usually filtered on campus.

Streaming podcasts and vidcasts that allow for interactivity will help make connections with other people and alleviate the potential isolation you may be struggling with in your situation. Podcasts and vidcasts also have value in archival material and static videos are found on TeacherTube or YouTube. For example UC Berkeley hosts a YouTube channel (http://www.youtube.com/ucberkeley) that covers courses, events, campus life, and athletics.

One of the flaws of streaming video is that they often take place during the school day. Also, the quality of the video and the sound can be suspect, although it is much improved. The value of archival material is the "just-in-time" nature of access and the ability to find what you need when you need it. However, viewing and listening to archived material does not allow for the interactivity that makes Web 2.0 tools so powerful in the learning arena. Exploring both live and archived materials will help a user determine the best source for personal learning.

A TOOL FOR SAVING AND SHARING

Have you ever seen a video and not saved it, or bookmarked it, only to want to return to it later? Vodpod (vodpod.com) is a social saving and sharing site for videos. Similar to social bookmarking sites, Vodpod allows you to install a toolbar button that when clicked upon, will save a video into your library. As a social networking site you can follow others and view what they are adding to their video library, as well as the tags they are using and their comments. It is a handy tool for gathering videos in one place with instant access from any computer, any time.

For true collaboration purposes, VoiceThread is an excellent tool. VoiceThread (http://voicethread.com) is a conversation centered on video. VoiceThread allows users to post video, audio, video and/or text comments on posted videos, and build conversation. It is a collaborative tool allowing asynchronous conversation in a global environment. It permits users to extend the conversation beyond their four walls and beyond their site-building relationships within the digital community.

The Internet has evolved into more than a textual and image-based environment. Increased bandwidth, open source, improved tools, and improved media have moved the digital environment into a true multimedia experience, complete with video, sound, and conversation, as well as the text, pictures, and photographs we are accustomed to using. New tools in the multimedia environment have improved our experiences in collaborating and learning in the global community if we maximize the use of such tools.

PODCAST SUGGESTIONS

Education Podcast Network (http://epnweb.org/index.php): This is a large directory of podcasts that is indexed by education (general theory), student and class projects, and subject-specific podcasts.

Education and Libraries

EdTech Weekly (http://www.edtechtalk.com/): This site hosts weekly shows that include *21st Century Learning, Women of Web 2.0, Teachers Teaching Teachers*, and so on.

Tech Chick Tips (http://techchicktips.net/podcast-episodes/): Tips found here focus on 21st-Century skills and integrating technology into the classroom.

Moving at the Speed of Creativity (http://www.speedofcreativity. org/): Wesley Fryer generally blogs and podcasts about improving student learning by integration of 21st-Century tools. He also examines Web 2.0 tools and the various ways they are being used.

YALSA (http://www.pod-serve.com/podcasts/show/yalsa-podcasts): The YALSA site focuses on library services for teens, including technology, programming, and literature.

EduCause (http://connect.educause.edu/podcasts): This site provides monthly podcasts focused on general education issues.

Literature and Books

HornBook Podcast (http://www.hbook.com/podcast/default.asp): Podcasts from HornBook offer conversations with authors, illustrators, and editors. The HornBook podcast will also discuss current trends in children's literature.

Booktalks—Quick and Simple (http://nancykeane.com/booktalks/ podcast.htm): Nancy Keane has made audio files of her booktalks, which range from children to young adult literature.

Lit2Go (http://etc.usf.edu/lit2go/): This is a collection of literary works recorded as MP3s. The works are primarily in the public domain and include classics such as *The Adventures of Huckleberry Finn*, and *Frankenstein.* It also includes poetry.

Comicpocalypse (http://www.comicpocalypse.com/): Although this is a growing podcast (as of August 2008), its 13 episodes are a funny, upbeat look at current comics.

iFanboy (http://www.thepodlounge.com.au/podcast/ifanboycom-comic-book-podcast): This is a more established podcast about the world of comics.

Book Bites for Kids (http://www.blogtalkradio.com/bookbitesforkids): From the National Writing for Children Center (http://writingforchildrencenter.com/), these podcasts feature interviews with children's authors.

Activated Stories (http://activated.libsyn.com/): Audio storytelling of children's stories are found on this site.

Large numbers of Harry Potter fan fiction and discussions can be found including harrypotterfanfiction, Sword of Gryffindor :: Hog's Head Pubcast, and so on. Twilight podcasts including Bloodsuckers, A Twilight PodCast, and Phases are also available.

News and Culture

Similar to blogs and Twitter accounts, most news organizations offer podcasts. CNN, NPR, and ABC have news podcasts. NPR also podcasts its radio shows, including Fresh Air, Talk of the Nation, This I Believe, and their StoryCorps project. *The New York Times* has podcasts connected to many of their section including the Front Page podcast, TimesTalk, and OpCast. *Slate*, the online webzine, also provides podcasts. Using iTunes, it is easy to find podcasts offered by your favorite news source or radio programs. This is true of sports media as well. ESPN offers a variety of podcasts from its radio shows, but there are other sports sources as well.

As in the literature genre podcasts, there are several podcasts that are fan-generated and related to popular television series and movies, including *Lost, Firefly/Serenity*, and *Heroes*.

Individual Podcasts

Grammar Girl (http://grammar.quickanddirtytips.com/): Even if you are not interested, English teachers might be.

American Experience (http://www.pbs.org/wgbh/amex/podcasts.html): Similar to Grammar Girl, this is to share with history teachers.

USA Today's Pop Candy Podcast (available through iTunes): This site offers a companion to the Pop Candy blog (http://blogs.usatoday.com/popcandy/).

Stuff You Should Know (available through iTunes): Connected to HowStuffWorks (howstuffworks.com), this is a weekly podcast of miscellanea.

The opportunities for learning online to expand your PLN are varied and exhaustive. Exploring the various formats can be both exciting and overwhelming. Finding the pieces to add to your network is not a weekend activity, it is ongoing, and your network will constantly change as you add and subtract individual sites, as well as tools. In the next chapter, I investigate information management tools and strategies for maintaining a healthy network.

CHAPTER 7
Managing the Information Flow

Since the 1980s, there has been a remarkable explosion in the amount of information readily available and content being created. With the introduction of Web 2.0 products in the past five years and the ability for people to easily create content and to collaborate and communicate in a global community, the access to, and creation of data has increased at a greater rate. The benefit of the read/write web, the ability to share information and experiences with easy tools across nations and around the globe is also the detriment of the read/write web. So much information and so many tools are available, and more are being added every day. How do you keep up? Plenty of tools are available to help you stay abreast of new offerings, but a more important skill is managing the information flow.

TOOLS

Tools help manage the information flow and help you organize the information, often in one place. If you have not yet read the section on RSS feeds, you need to go back and do that before you continue. A feed aggregator is an invaluable tool in organizing the updates of information that will cross your computer screen. Other information aggregate managers to consider include iGoogle, Pageflakes, and NetVibes. All of these tools are personalized home pages that allow a user to add individual items that bring together the multiple tools we use in the information economy. For example, on Pageflakes you can add feeds, keep a calendar, download your e-mail, host your Delicious bookmarks, and share your PageCasts with others. The same is true in iGoogle, although you cannot share your iGoogle pages. The Google tool suite is easier to add, so if you rely heavily on the Google tools, it may be a preferable home page.

NetVibes is similar to the other two, only prettier, so if design is important to you and you are comfortable in the NetVibes environment, it may be your choice. In each of the three tools you can add other pages that show up as "tabs." This is helpful in differentiating between tools, e-mail addresses, feeds, and accounts that you maintain for professional rather than personal needs. You also can use tabs to arrange your information by content (i.e., Library, Ed-Tech, Reading). Designing a personal home page that you can designate as your home page on computers you use regularly can be quite a bit of fun, and is an excellent tool in information management.

Information Management Tools

Second Brain (http://secondbrain.com/): Collect and share files, Web content, and social networking accounts.

Alerts.com (www.alerts.com/): Need a reminder? Sign up for alerts that are sent to your desktop, e-mail, or phone.

Fuser (https://www.fuser.com/): Collects all e-mail accounts, Facebook/MySpace updates, and Twitter feeds.

Another information management tool to consider is an e-mail aggregator. GMail (Google's e-mail tool) is an example of an e-mail aggregator that integrates chat, a calendar, and RSS alerts, as well as downloading messages from different e-mail accounts. Several other e-mail aggregators include a variety of tools. Zenbe is an excellent example. It allows users to combine all the e-mail addresses (and Facebook) they use into one place and create and share lists. It provides a calendar tool, file-upload capacity, and stores attachments separately so the user can search just attachments rather than sifting through e-mails. A visit to mashable (http://mashable.com/) will provide other e-mail aggregating tools.

PERSONAL LEARNING NETWORK: COLLECTION DEVELOPMENT

A PLN is a collection of resources, and similar to a library collection is most useful if it is well maintained. It can be overwhelming, and you may find yourself behind on reading, listening, and viewing. You may find that you have added too many resources to thoughtfully follow any of the frequently updated pages, posts, and tweets. While maintaining a PLN, the best thing you can do is spend time using a wide variety of tools, searching for a diversity of sources; but as you get comfortable in your network or as your needs change, you may find yourself needing to "weed" your PLN. Strategies and organization for maintaining a PLN will develop over time but there are some strategies that will help with network upkeep.

1. Use your aggregator to organize feeds into folders that make sense to you. You can organize them by importance, by subject, by urgency, or by frequency. However you organize your feeds, do not be afraid to reorganize them if it isn't working.

2. Weed your feeds. Pay close attention to which feeds you read regularly, and those you may chose to skip if your time is limited. Are there some you never read? Or a feed that is no longer updating? Are there topics that you are no longer interested in? Delete feeds to keep your network of a reasonable size, which only you can determine.

3. Add feeds of blog searches or alerts for topics that you may be interested in for a short amount of time and delete when it is no longer of use. If it is a unit used every year add the relevant sites to the social bookmarking tool that you use.

4. When you have a network that is a reasonable size you may wish to implement a "closet rule." If you add one feed, take one out.

5. Scan and save. Not every post needs thoughtful, deep reading. In fact many articles, posts, and links that appear in your aggregator can be scanned. If you wish to spend time reading an article, post or save it in your aggregator until you have the time and space to concentrate on what you are reading.

6. Purge. Have you gotten behind? Does the number of new items in your aggregator overwhelm you? Don't be afraid to purge without interacting with all the information.

7. Unplug. We all need a break, take one.

For further examination of managing your PLN visit Jeff Utecht's excellent post at http://www.thethinkingstick.com/?p=652 which examines the stages of PLN development.

Managing a PLN is about balance and discovering which tools and networks work for you, which listservs you can manage, which sites you'll visit, which feeds you read, learn, and enjoy. Each person's network will work differently, will include personalized information, and will take different amounts of time. It is essential to know yourself. Can you turn off and walk away? Can you delete without reading? How much time can you spend? How do you learn best? Answering those questions will help identify which tools, networks, and people you should include in your learning experiences.

Glossary

AASL: American Association of School Librarians. *The mission of the American Association of School Librarians is to advocate excellence, facilitate change, and develop leaders in the school library media field.* (http://www.ala.org/ala/aasl/aboutaasl/missionandgoals/aaslmissiongoals.cfm)

ACRL: Association of College and Research Libraries.

Advocacy: Webster's defines advocacy as "the act or process of advocating or supporting a cause or proposal." In school libraries advocacy is an essential job responsibility. We describe, enlist support, and speak for our programs and our students to parents, administrators, school boards, legislators, and various other decision makers.

Aggregator: A term used for software that gathers data from a variety of sources into one place. Usually refers to news readers, or feed readers which gather syndicated content.

ALA: American Library Association.

ALSC: Association for Library Services to Children.

Asynchronous: Allows for submitting data to Web pages without resubmitting the whole page. Also references conversations occurring in which comments occur at different times, again without requiring resubmission of the entire Web page.

Avatar: A digitized representation of self; can be a recognizable 3-D object or an icon.

Best practice: The concept that a methodology or approach will lead to the best result; in education the result that optimizes student achievement.

Blog: Derived from Weblog. Blogs are Web pages that are updated frequently, generally created by an individual. They contain text, images, videos, and are a fundamental part of the Internet, a ubiquitous piece of the World Wide Web.

Blogger: One who writes a blog.

Blogroll: A collection of links to blogs hosted on a blog page, usually to blogs the hosting blogger reads.

Bloom's taxonomies: A classification of levels of intellectual activities: includes knowledge, understanding, application, analysis, synthesis, and evaluation.

Continuing Education Units: Offered through universities and organizations these are classes designed to further your learning, and often offer college course units, which meet requirements for credential renewals in some states, and some district employment requirements.

Creative Commons: An organization designed to fill the gaps in copyright law and provide greater flexibility. It is possible to license work under a creative commons license that allow for a range of attribution and derivation possibilities. Many digital sites use Creative Commons licenses. (http://creativecommons.org/)

Critical Literacy: Adopts a critical and questioning approach to texts. It includes examining the explicit and implicit meaning of a text, examining the text relation to other texts, examining the methods used to construct a text, and emphasizes multiple readings. Critical literacy and information literacy have many attributes in common surrounding analysis and evaluation of a text.

Effective Practice: Similar to best practices; practice based on evidence over an extended time that produces desired results.

Feed Readers: Software that aggregates RSS content.

Folksonomy: User generated keywords designed to describe content, a community, collaborative taxonomy.

Guided Learning: An online course that offers an instructor, assignments, and specific deadlines, as well as the possibility of instructor/student interaction in real time.

Hyperlinks: Links to another Web site or page within a site.

Icon: A picture that represents a command, person, object, etc.

Information aggregate managers: Web based software that uses widgets, and RSS, to pull all of your information into one place.

ISTE: International Society for Technology in Education. *"Providing leadership and service to improve teaching and learning by advancing the effective use of technology in education."* (http://www.iste.org)

Kidlitosphere: The blogging community that focuses on children's and young adult literature.

Killer App: Short for killer application in today's computer jargon, it refers to a popular application that changes common processes, revolutionizes the tasks people complete regularly, and is often seen as the one application people cannot do without.

Library 2.0: Based on the concepts of Web 2.0 and Business 2.0, Library 2.0 focuses on user input, collaboration with the user community, 24/7 digital delivery of content that emphasizes interaction with users.

Listservs: A collection of members who have signed up to communicate with one another using e-mail.

Literacy: There are several different identified literacies. Literacy is the catch all term for the ability to read, write, and communicate. Below are the specific definitions of some of the literacies teacher-librarians are likely to encounter.

- **Basic Literacy or Functional Literacy**: the ability to read, write, and communicate.

- **Information Literacy** has been defined as "the ability to access, evaluate, and use information from a variety of sources." (Doyle March/April 1995)

- The New Media Consortium defined **21st Century Literacy** in 2005 as "the set of abilities and skills where aural visual and digital literacy overlap" "the ability to understand the power of images and sounds, to recognize and use that power, to manipulate and transform digital media, to distribute them persuasively, and to easily adapt them to new forms."

- David Buckingham in his 2003 book *Media Literacy* defined **media literacy** thusly: "refers to knowledge skills, and competencies that are required in order to use and interpret media." It is a "form of critical literacy, involves analysis, evaluation, and critical reflection."

- Based on NETS developed and released in 2007 by ISTE, **ICT literacy** incorporates the concepts of Creativity and Innovation, Communication and Collaboration, Research and Information Fluency, Critical Thinking, Problem Solving, and Decision Making, Digital Citizenship, and Technology Concepts and Operation. Similar to Information Literacy, ICT literacy is an evolving concept, just recently moving beyond the ability to merely use the hardware and software of computer systems.

Literacy coaches: Teachers who support classroom teachers in implementing effective literacy practices and teaching methodologies in the classroom.

Lurk: The practice of reading postings or e-mails with out posting yourself.

Mash-up: Content or an application that uses or combines data from multiple sources.

Media Literacy: The process of synthesizing, and using, different forms of mass media. The skills in media literacy have connections to information literacy including the ability to analyze, synthesize, and evaluate information.

Memes: The actual definition of a meme is a unit of culture, or an idea that is repeated throughout a culture. In the blogosphere it generally refers to a questionnaire or a "fill in the blank" blog post that circulates throughout blog connections, similar to a chain letter.

NCLB: No Child Left Behind. Federal legislation guiding education policy that requires highly qualified teachers, and stresses improved student achievement, generally defined by achievement on high stakes multiple choice standardized tests based on curricular standards in the four core curriculum: Language Arts, Math, Social Science, and Science.

NCTE: National Council of Teachers of English.

NSFW: An acronym used by bloggers to refer to sites and posts that are Not Safe For Work.

Open Source: Generally speaking this applies to software which makes code available for modification, and the ability to produce software that adds to the original.

Podcast: A digital broadcast of sound, generally spoken word—similar to a radio show.

Push technology: Subscription services in which information is delivered to the end user by the host.

Read Write Web: There are subtle linguistics differences between Read Write Web and Web 2.0 based on the history of use but in this book it is synonmous with Web 2.0.

RSS: Real Simple Syndication. The standard that allows for syndication of Web content that provides for easy, frequent updates and distribution.

SMS blogging: Short Message Service blogging. Primarily status updates, generally 140 characters or less.

Social Networking: Digital network of friends hosted on the Web.

Social Web: A reference to the collaborative nature of Web 2.0; another term for Web 2.0.

Syndicated Content: Content from a site updated regularly without end user intervention.

Tag: A keyword used to describe content of a Web site, blog entry, or other syndicated content.

Tag Cloud: A visual representation of a user's tags.

Taxonomy: Codified subject terms, or controlled vocabulary.

Teacher-Librarians: There is often a debate about "what we call ourselves." I choose teacher-librarian to reflect a person with a certification or with a master's degree in Library and Information Science working in a school library. We are also known as school librarians, library media specialists or teachers, and media specialists.

Texting: The practice of sending short written messages via phone.

Thread: A series of e-mails on one particular topic.

Tweens: An age range generally referred to as ages 10–14.

Virtual Environment: An ecology that exists in the digital world.

Vlog: A video blog.

Vodcast: A video version of a podcast, posted video blogs or vlogs.

Web 2.0: This generally applies to the newer developments in the Internet that allow for greater collaboration, easier user created content, and increased information sharing. It encapsulates a range of tools that allow for increased creativity, communication, and sharing.

Webcast: Posting/sending live video or audio content via the Web.

Webinar: A webcast designed for learning.

Widget: A software application that interacts with hosting software to display information.

Wikis: A user edited Web page that encourages user content and editing.

YALSA: Young Adult Library Services Association. The mission is to *"to advocate, promote and strengthen service to young adults as part of the continuum of total library service, and to support those who provide service to this population."* (http://www.ala.org/ala/yalsa/aboutyalsab/yalsamission.cfm)

Youth Divisions: Refers to the divisions of ALA that service youth: AASL, ALSC, and YALSA.

Index

About the Author

MARY ANN HARLAN is a librarian at Arcata High School, Northern Humboldt Union High School District, Arcata, California.